The Lord of the Psalms

The Lord of the Psalms

Patrick D. Miller

WESTMINSTER
JOHN KNOX PRESS
LOUISVILLE · KENTUCKY

© 2013 Patrick D. Miller

First edition
Published by Westminster John Knox Press
Louisville, Kentucky

13 14 15 16 17 18 19 20 21 22—10 9 8 7 6 5 4 3 2 1

Unless otherwise identified, Scripture quotations are from the New Revised Standard Version of the Bible, copyright © 1989 by the Division of Christian Education of the National Council of the Churches of Christ in the U.S.A., and used by permission. Any emphasis is added. Texts marked AT are the author's translation. Verses marked NJPS are from *Tanakh: The Holy Scriptures: The New JPS Translation according to the Traditional Hebrew Text,* © 1985, 1999 by The Jewish Publication Society; all rights reserved; used by permission.

Book design by Sharon Adams
Cover design by Dilu Nicholas
Cover illustration: Park in a fog © *Triff/shutterstock.com;*
Abstract orange background © *Attitude/shutterstock.com*

Library of Congress Cataloging-in-Publication Data
is on file at the Library of Congress, Washington, DC.

ISBN: 978-0-664-23927-5

♾ The paper used in this publication meets the minimum requirements
of the American National Standard for Information Sciences—Permanence
of Paper for Printed Library Materials, ANSI Z39.48-1992.

Most Westminster John Knox Press books are available at special quantity discounts when purchased in bulk by corporations, organizations, and special-interest groups. For more information, please e-mail SpecialSales@wjkbooks.com.

To
Thomas W. Gillespie
1928–2011

Contents

Acknowledgments

The chapters of this book are largely adapted from the Stone Lectures delivered in October 2010 at Princeton Theological Seminary. Knowing how the Stone Lecturers are chosen, I am keenly aware of the responsibility (or blame) that rests upon members of the Department of Biblical Studies for their leadership in the decision that led to my invitation. It is fitting, therefore, that I say what will always be a part of my life at Princeton Seminary. It is not possible for me to imagine a happier, friendlier, or more supportive group of teacher-scholars than my colleagues/friends in the Department of Biblical Studies. The two things that remain most with me from over twenty years of teaching at Princeton Seminary are the joy of helping prepare men and women for the ministry and the pleasant context for doing that provided by all my colleagues, but especially those with whom I worked in the teaching of Scripture. These lectures are an all-too-modest way of saying thank-you to each of them for that gift.

There are many others who have aided me in thinking about the subject matter of these lectures, including thoughtful comments and questions from colleagues and friends on the occasion of delivering them. I also received helpful assistance in thinking through and formulating my thoughts from a longtime friend and fellow interpreter of the Old Testament, Gerald Janzen.

My years of teaching coincided closely with the time Tom Gillespie served as President of Princeton Seminary. His leadership and friendship were also a gift that I can never forget. No one could have been more supportive of my teaching and my scholarship than he was. I owe him a debt that could never have been repaid. It is a sad joy to be able to dedicate the publication of the Stone Lectures in his honor and to his memory.

Introduction

In his introduction to a translation of the Psalms, Martin Luther called the book of Psalms, or the Psalter, "eine kleine Biblia," a small Bible. It was a simple way of identifying the breadth and comprehensiveness of the Psalms as a testimony to God's way with us in the world God created. The genres and settings in life of the Psalms tend to focus our attention on the human worshiper and the worshiper's context, whether one of dire straits or of joyous worship. For most of the Psalter, the one who speaks in the Psalms is the human creature, not the divine Creator. As that happens, we learn much about that creature as we listen to these different voices, often echoing each other in their cries for help and in their hymns of praise.[1]

Still, all these prayers and songs are directed toward or in response to the Lord, whose care of the psalmist(s) and of the world the psalmist inhabits is the presupposition of every psalm. From beginning to end, the subject matter of the Psalms is the Lord of Israel. In various ways the many lament psalms or prayers for help that are so pervasive in the Psalter speak to and about God; in so doing they inform the one reading them of what this God is like and why one turns in that direction in times of trouble. Whether in the various ascriptions and pleas that seek to arouse the Lord's response or in the expressions of confidence and assurance, the one who cries out informs us about the one being addressed and the reader or pray-er of the psalms engages in the theological task but via the genre of prayer. What happens is what always happens in prayer: a theological understanding of the One to whom the prayer is lifted is both implicit and explicit in the prayer. We learn about God as we pray. We say what we know and believe about God as we cry out. That is certainly the case with the psalmist.

As much or even more is the case with the many hymns and songs of thanksgiving present in the Psalter. While their intent is to call members of the community to the praise of God ("Hallelujah! Praise the LORD!") or to acknowledge and give thanks for God's help ("O give thanks to the LORD") the hymns and songs are filled with all the reasons why praise and thanksgiving to this God are appropriate and necessary, as in the paradigmatic short thanksgiving:

O give thanks to the LORD, for he is good;
    for his steadfast love endures forever. (Ps. 107:1)

Also, in the several songs of trust (e.g., Pss. 23; 27), the psalmist elaborates at length on aspects of God's being and way that elicit trust, even in the worst of circumstances.

So it is that whether in prayer or in song, in loneliness and isolation or in community and worship, the Psalms bear constant testimony to the Lord of Israel and in so doing tell us in full measure who and what this God is. While we learn much about ourselves as we listen to and meditate on the Psalms, in a far more abundant manner we learn about the Lord. What follows in this book is an effort to explore pieces of that "information" as a way of learning more about the One we worship on the way to our own prayer and praise. In some cases this exploration is focused on particular psalms; in others it is more a wide-ranging survey as a particular theological topic is examined through the lens of various psalms. Because this book arises out of the Stone Lectures delivered at Princeton Theological Seminary in 2010, it is in ways more probing than comprehensive or systematic, spotting places where theological issues arise and are addressed, but not in itself a full theology of the Psalms.

What is self-evident for any effort at some thematic study of the Psalms is that one may—and probably should—approach the material in several ways. That is, the interpreter whose attention is focused on a particular topic or theme is bound at some point to want to pursue that theme through the whole of the Psalter, such as via language and genre. But often a particular psalm may quite dramatically or profoundly open up a particular topic or subject in a way that does not exclude other texts but offers a focused way into the subject. Further, it has become quite common in contemporary study of the Psalms to look at the Psalter as a whole and see both interconnections between particular psalms in the way in which they are ordered and arranged and things of significance in the movement of the Psalter as a whole. All of these avenues are evident in the pages that follow.

My starting point is the very basic question about the reality of God in the world in which these prayers are prayed. In a biblical book where God is the chief subject and addressee, the question about God's true presence in the world is raised in genuine and radical fashion, but in such a way that the answer to the question is both a matter of evidence and also of decision. Nor in this context can one avoid some attention to the knowledge of God, both how we know and how we are known.

In a quite different way the question of God is raised by one of the most interesting and unusual psalms in the Psalter. The short Psalm 82, not one of the psalms most often read or memorized, makes a judgment about what constitutes deity. The psalm makes one of the most startling claims in the literature of the ancient world: that all the gods of heaven have been stripped of their deity and mortalized by Elohim/God. The reason for such an unbelievable conclusion is clear in the story that unfolds in this psalm.

How the Psalms speak about God and portray the Lord of the Psalms is a large factor in their theology. The primary sense one has of the God-talk of the Psalms is the degree to which God is embodied and personalized. This is manifest in various categories: body, name, voice and speech, space and place, and temporality. Such language does not exhaust the way in which we encounter God in the Psalms, but it stands at the center of their portrayal and makes the reader less surprised to encounter the Word made flesh when we meet him in the New Testament.

One of the most repeated epithets to characterize the Lord of the Psalms is "maker of heaven and earth." While Genesis commands our primary attention when asking about creation and the Creator, one should not skip over the Psalms in this regard. Not only is much attention given to God's work of creation, but it also comes to us in a quite different mode than what we encounter in Genesis. The language of poetry provides a different vehicle for thinking and speaking about creation, one less vulnerable to tensions and conflicts with other modes of thinking about how our world came to be. Further, the Psalms make it clear that creation is not an isolated or finished event. Whether one calls it continuous creation or providence, it is clear that the celebration of God as Creator is not tied to the past or the beginning alone. The completeness of creation that seems to be so clear in Genesis is not to be downplayed. But it must be held in tension with all the indications in the Psalms that the earth is still the Lord's and its ongoing nurture is the context in which all the power of God in behalf of the weak and the poor and the oppressed is manifest.

Among the interpretive directions reflected in these pages is the way in which particular psalms can so largely convey the fundamental message of the whole, or at least reveal some of the most basic convictions about the Lord of the Psalms that one finds in the whole of Scripture. One of those particular psalms is Psalm 86, explored in these pages to see how the prayers of the Psalter tell us about the God to whom they are prayed and particularly how they are varied articulations of the character of God's steadfast love and compassion.

A rich example of the power of the individual psalm to proclaim who and what God is like and how the Lord rules and cares is Psalm 103. It has captured the hearts of countless people through the ages by its compassionate, realistic, and unflinching portrait of God's way with us and the world in which we live. To explore its manifold dimensions is to be given access to the grace that is the ground of all our hope and consolation.

Although one may find individual psalms encapsulating much of what we need to know and hear and say about the Lord of the Psalms, it is also true that every psalm is to be read and heard in its context. The Psalter is a book, and as such it provides a setting for every psalm, and every psalm is to be read not simply as an individual piece of poetry, prayer, or praise but also as related to and connecting with other psalms around it or elsewhere in the book. And as a book it provides us with a holistic text and not just a collection of individual, separate, and unrelated pieces. To hear the Psalms in their fullness is to listen to them as a whole, hearing the many resonances among them as well as discerning the different ways of reading the Psalter as a whole. As one way of doing that, the final chapter of the book seeks to explore how the Psalter serves to give us an exposition of the answer to the first question of the Westminster Shorter Catechism: "What is the chief end of man?"

My learning of the Bible began with the Psalms. They continue to provide the voice I need to hear and to speak. Listening to them to learn more fully about the God we worship is the ultimate goal of this book. It is my hope that these chapters serve also as a moment of praise and thanksgiving to the Lord of the Psalms.

Chapter One

The Reality of God

Years ago, just before I began my teaching ministry, Mary Ann and I spent several months in Israel. During that time I would regularly walk down the street to a news vendor, buy a copy of *Time* magazine, and try to catch up with the world news and what was going on back home. I can still remember the day in April—it was the Easter season—when I made my usual walk to get the weekly copy; as I picked it up, I was quite taken aback. There was—for the first time in the history of the magazine—no picture on the cover. Instead there was only a black cover with the words "Is God Dead?"[1]

I was not the only person startled at this Easter cover. That cover and the accompanying story received more reader response than any story in the history of the magazine to that point—at least a sign that theological issues are not unimportant to many people. I expect it was also an indication that the issue posed in the question and the discussion of it touched a nerve in many people, Christian and non-Christian, persons who believe in God and persons who do not.

The article reflected an extensive theological debate going on in the 1960s as to whether God or the notion of God—and both ways of putting the matter were in view—is dead. That debate, widely publicized in a way not usually the case for theological matters, is past, at least as a public phenomenon and item of news. But the question raised and the claims asserted in the debate have been around for a long time in some form or another, and they still persist among many persons as nagging but serious questions. Is God a reality, one with which we have to deal, or not? Is God real?

1

The Psalms are so clear and articulate, so frequent and expansive in their praise and proclamation of the Lord and the Lord's way, that it may seem to be an unasked or irrelevant question as to whether or not God is real and present in the world. At the same time, it might be argued that nowhere else in the Bible does one find questions about that reality so frequent and articulate and so tied to the human condition as in the Psalms. Of course, the customary place for pursuit of this issue is usually in either Job or Ecclesiastes, and not without good reason. What is particularly noticeable or characteristic of the Psalms is the juxtaposition of the extravagant claims and the deep doubts—often in verses right next to each other—doubts not raised in intellectual reflection but in the depths of despair and anguish. It seems appropriate, therefore, to begin our thinking about the Lord of the Psalms by seeing how and why the psalmist confronts the reality of God and what that engagement contributes to our understanding of the theology of the Psalms. I am going to do that via two theological issues: the existence of God and the knowledge of God.

The Existence of God

As a way into the matter, let us look at the perspectives of three different groups represented or illustrated in different psalms but clearly interacting with one another. Those different groups are (1) the foolish, the group least present in an explicit sense in the Psalms, but they are there; (2) the enemy or the wicked, and they are hard to distinguish and often present; and (3) the suffering praying one, whose voice is probably the loudest and most widespread of any other.

If we start with the fool, the *nābāl*, we encounter a member of the community well known in Proverbs and elsewhere but less present in the Psalms. In fact, the *nābāl* appears in only four psalms [14 = 53; 39; 74]. In two of them, Psalms 39 and 74, the fool is identified as one who utters scorn or scoff (*ḥerpâ*). In Psalm 39, the praying one says: "Deliver me from all my transgressions. Do not make me the scorn of the fool" (v. 8). In Psalm 74, one of the community laments that complains to God over the absence of divine intervention to help the people against a powerful enemy, the fool appears twice, once as "a foolish nation," that is, the enemy (vv. 18 AT, 22). And the scoffing or taunting is mentioned a third time, again with reference to the enemy. In Psalm 39 the scoffing is directed toward the suffering psalmist. Psalm 74, however, has each instance referring to scorning or taunting God. Ultimately there is no difference, it would seem, particularly when we ask, What is the nature of this taunt or the scoffing voice of the fool, who is seen to be an echo of what the enemy says, and vice versa? The clearest answer to that comes from the one other psalm where the fool appears. It is Psalm 14 [= 53] with its familiar opening verse: "Fools say in their hearts, 'There is no God.'" That such an assumption is at the heart of the taunt of fool and enemy is confirmed when one hears the psalmist in Psalm 42 complain: "My adversaries *taunt* me, while they say to me continually, 'Where is your God?'" (v. 10). Likewise in Psalm 10 the praying one says:

> In the pride of their countenance the wicked say,
>> "God will not seek it out";
> All their thoughts are, "There is no God." (v. 4)

The fool is not finally different from the enemy or from the wicked. In both instances, the taunt against God is a conviction, a view of reality that is held within the heart and mind. Several times in Psalm 10, one of the powerful complaint psalms of the Psalter, we hear what the wicked/ enemy/fool really believes in the heart (vv. 6, 11, 13). We shall come back to these, but first a look at the basic conviction of the fool = wicked. "There is no god" is not a philosophical or ontological statement. Thus *'ēn 'ĕlōhîm* means simply God is not present, God is not here (10:4). When we read that "Sarah was barren" (*'ēn lāh wālād*, Gen. 11:30), the text simply tells us she had no child. Children were abundant, but not with Sarah. Similarly, *'ēn kesep* means "There is no money," but the point is that the speaker doesn't have any. So the fool's claim is that God is not around and need not be accounted for.

After that initial assumption or conviction, Psalm 14 goes on as follows:

> They are corrupt, they do abominable deeds;
>> there is no one who does good.
> The Lord looks down from heaven on humankind
>> to see if there are any who are wise,
>> who seek after God.
> They have all gone astray, they are all alike perverse;
>> there is no one who does good,
>> no, not one.
> Have they no knowledge, all the evildoers
>> who eat up my people as they eat bread,
>> and do not call upon the Lord? (vv. 1b–4)

It is clear why the foolish one says in her heart, "There is no God." It is because there is total corruption, nothing but abominable deeds. There are only evil and injustice. There are *none* that "seek after God," an expression that surely must be understood in the context of the prophetic message of Amos, where the people are called to "seek the LORD and live," an instruction that is then spelled out: "Seek good and not evil, that you may live," and "Hate evil and love good, and establish justice in the gate," that is, in the courts (5:14–15). So also Psalm 24 describes the "company of those who *seek him*" as "those who have clean hands and pure hearts, who do not lift up their souls to what is false, and do not swear deceitfully" (vv. 4, 6). As the basis for the fool's claim that there is no God, Psalm 14 sets the evidence that there is no good or that there is no one who does good. In other words, no good means no god.

The point is underscored in spades in the interior thoughts of the wicked in Psalm 10:

> "He [God] does not call to account." . . .
> "There is no God." (v. 4 AT)
> They [the wicked] say in their heart,
> "I shall never be shaken, (v. 6a AT)
> through all time never be in trouble." (v. 6b NJPS)
> They [the wicked] say in their heart, (v. 11a AT)
> "God has forgotten, he has hidden his face, he will never see it."
> (v. 11b)
> Why do the wicked renounce God,
> and say in their hearts,
> "You will not call us to account?" (v. 13)

What is clear from both psalms is that the claim "There is no God" or "God is not here" arises on two grounds:

1. All the indications that God is *not present*. That is, God is hidden, God's face *is hidden*, God is nowhere around. God has forgotten. God does not see. God hides. God stands afar off: "Your judgments are on high, out of their sight." (Ps. 10:5; various of these expressions occurring in the two psalms).
2. God is either *not powerful* in the situation or does not exercise any power to do anything in the face of wickedness, evil, oppression, and injustice. "You will not call *to account*." "Through all time I shall never be in trouble," says the fool or wicked. God does not

do anything against the wicked to stop the evil or the wicked. The conclusion therefore is obvious: For all intents and purposes, there is no God.

What I think we hear in these psalms and elsewhere is that the question about God—or the assumption of no God, God is gone, dead, and so forth—was very real in Israel. That question is present in the questions of the psalmic complaint prayers as at the beginning of Psalm 13:

> How long, O LORD? Will you forget me forever?
>   How long will you hide your face from me?
> How long must I bear pain in my soul?
>   and have sorrow in my heart all day long?
> How long shall my enemy be exalted over me?

In Psalms 14 and 53 and Psalm 10, however, the wicked or foolish have no questions about God. They already know the answer. They have worked it out pragmatically, scientifically, in a sense. Look at the evidence. They are able to carry out their evil and oppressive deeds without anything happening to them. No one is there to call them to account.

> Their ways prosper at all times. (10:5)
> They seize the poor and drag them off in their net.
> They stoop, they crouch,
>   and the helpless fall by their might. (10:9–10)

Or in Psalm 94:6–7:

> They kill the widow and the stranger,
>   they murder the orphan,
> and they say, "The LORD does not see."

It would be a mistake, however, to take these assumptions about God's absence and noninvolvement as confined to the interior thoughts of wicked and foolish persons who get away with murder (literally and metaphorically). The psalms we are talking about are either all or in part *laments*. They are cries for help and expressions of Israelites' despair and anguish before God in the face of oppression and injustice. That the question about God and God's reality was not confined to the foolish and wicked is evident in several ways.

1. The depiction of the human situation in Psalm 14—"They are corrupt. . . . There is no one who does good, no, not a single one" (vv. 1, 4 AT)—is as much the perception of the *psalmist* as it is of the fool or wicked. It is the psalmist who sees a situation where evil runs rampant, where there is no sign of the presence of God and no resistance to the total evil that suggests the presence and power of God.

2. Second, we need to recognize that the many quotations of the thoughts and the words of the wicked and foolish in these prayer psalms are a way of indirectly expressing the conclusions of the psalmist herself in the face of the reality of the current situation. As Rolf Jacobson has noted in his study of the quotations in the Psalms, "The psalmist could *quote* the enemy [as] uttering genuine assertions of God's powerlessness because the act of quoting dissociates the psalmist from the responsibility for this assertion."[2] Implicitly they are what the psalmist sees as well but does not express so directly.

3. Still, and this is where the psalmist's own voice comes into the picture, the sentiments articulated so directly and crassly in the thoughts of the wicked and foolish come to life in the words of the psalmists, but they do so in direct address to God, both in questions and in challenges. Thus in letting go of God, the psalmist does not let go of God. In Psalm 42, the psalmist says: "I say to God, my rock, 'Why have you forgotten me?'" followed by the words "My adversaries taunt me, while they say to me continually, 'Where is your God?'" (vv. 9–10). The *interior thought* of the wicked in Psalm 10, "God has forgotten," becomes a *question to God* on the part of the psalmist in Psalm 42: "Why have you forgotten me?" The communal prayer of Psalm 74 begins, "O God, why do you cast us off forever?" and later says: "How long, O God, is the foe to scoff?" (vv. 1, 10). And we know what that scoffing is all about. Perhaps nowhere does the human challenge and question to and about God arise more thoroughly than in Psalm 22, where the suffering psalmist is mocked by others who say: "Commit your cause to the LORD; let him deliver—let him rescue the one in whom he delights!" (v. 8). But it is in the psalmist's own words at the beginning that we hear the fool's assumption about the reality of God raised in the questions of the psalmist, the starting point here: "My God, my God, why have you forsaken me? Why are you so far from helping me, from the words of my groaning? O my God, I cry by day, but you do not answer; and by night but find no rest" (vv. 1–2). If the cries of the psalmists in their suffering are "out of the depths," as we hear in Psalm 130 (v. 1), nowhere are the depths any deeper or farther away than the voice we hear in Psalm 22. The psalmist's experience is

turned into questions. God has abandoned the supplicant. God is utterly gone, far away. Why? Where? There is no sound, no answer to the questions, no word from the Lord of any sort. God is uninvolved, not here, not present. That is the experience and sense of the psalmist. And while there are many texts that flow from the Old Testament into the New, surely none is more important than this text and its locus on the lips of the incarnate One, the Word become flesh, God in our midst and one of us, whose own experience raises all the questions of human existence about the reality of God.

So the question about God that is so apparent in the words and acts of the wicked and foolish is raised also on the part of believers, who uttered their prayers for help, the largest genre of psalms in the Psalter. In the face of the evidence and in their own way, they asked the question that was asked of them: "Where is God?" And the nature of the theistic question as it arises in these psalms is indeed a question about whether God is present in the human situation and whether God has power to do anything about the human situation. It is also clearly a moral issue. What we encounter are both assumptions and painful questions about whether there is any reality to God. Does God make any difference where the difference counts, that is, in the face of human need and human oppression? The questions are not philosophical or ontological, but they are the bottom line, the ones that matter. The taunting and scoffing are real, symbolized in the question of the wicked or of the enemies that becomes the question of the one in trouble: "Where is your God?" And it is cast at the one in trouble because there is no sign of God with such a one. In Matthew 27 we hear the following words: "In the same way the chief priests also, along with the scribes and elders, were mocking him, saying, . . . 'He trusts in God; let God deliver him now'" (vv. 41–43). The deep association of Psalm 22 with the suffering and death of Jesus is no accident. It puts the issue of God's reality at the center of the Christian story. It may be the deepest clue to the meaning of the incarnation. He was "born in human likeness" (Phil. 2:7), beset by evil and wickedness, suffering and asking, "Where is God? Why is God not here if there is a God?"

Thus the Psalms make it very clear that the large human questions about the reality, existence, and presence of God are not a modern phenomenon. From the beginning they were deeply present in the midst of the community of faith. Our awareness of that is crucial, for such uncertainty about the reality and presence and power of God is not all that we encounter, even in those psalms where the doubts are the weightiest.

The foolish and the wicked draw their conclusion from the facts: when the innocent are done in, nothing happens to rectify the situation. It may be a useful conclusion for the fool because it means that he or she can go ahead with their oppressive deeds with impunity, or without having to worry about any accountability. Both the wicked and the righteous *see the data*—the absence of any doer of good, the hapless falling at the hands of the wicked—both see this evidence yet end up drawing different conclusions; this fact means that the matter is not simply a judgment forced on one by the evidence. It is indeed *also a choice*, that is, *bad faith*. For many if not most of these prayers for help that lay out the evidence do go on not only to appeal to and petition God but also to make powerful claims *against the apparent evidence*.

Thus in Psalm 14—even after the devastating picture of the human situation as a place where "they are all alike perverse, there is no one who does good, not a single one" (v. 3 AT), and where the evildoers "eat up my people like bread"—we hear these words: "God is with the company of the righteous. You would confound the plans of the poor, but the LORD is their refuge" (vv. 6–7). And in Psalm 10, after the psalmist quotes the interior thoughts of the wicked, "God has forgotten, he has hidden his face, he will never see it" (v. 11), the supplicant goes on to say, "But you do see! Indeed you note trouble and grief, that you may take it into your hands" (v. 14). The psalmist who in Psalm 42 says, "Why have you forgotten me?" precedes that complaint with the words, "I say to God, my rock" (v. 9). And in Psalm 22, those "Why" questions of one for whom God is absent and silent are preceded by the exclamation "My God, my God," the most personal and repeated claim of a relationship that we have in the whole Psalter. For the Psalms, that is where life is lived: between the deeply personal claim "my God, my God," and the experience of abandonment, absence, and silence that is often the human experience. And before Psalm 22 is over, we will hear the words, "You have answered me" (v. 21 AT), followed by what I would call the most powerful song of thanksgiving in all of Scripture:

> I will tell of your name to my brothers and sisters;
>   in the midst of the congregation I will praise you;
> You who fear the LORD, praise him!
>   All you offspring of Jacob, glorify him;
>   stand in awe of him, all you offspring of Israel! (vv. 22–23)

And this song of praise goes on for ten verses!

How can we take these claims seriously if we do not find in the midst of them the questions that belong to our faith and experience in conversation with one another and in the world we inhabit? But if our uncertainty about the power and presence of God in our midst is an echo of the questions of those who prayed these prayers, then it may be possible for us to join them also in the claims and assumptions about God to which they held, even in the face of such God-denying experiences. The questions are not apart from a deep trust in the one whose absence and silence are not the final words.

We should note one further dimension of the issue, especially as it appears in Psalm 14. Attend to verses 1–3 one more time:

> Fools says in their hearts, "There is no God."
>> They are corrupt, they do abominable deeds;
>> there is no one who does good.
> The LORD looks down from heaven on humankind
>> to see if there are any who are wise,
>> who seek after God.
> They have all gone astray, they are all alike perverse;
>> there is no one who does good, no, not one.

A counterperspective is evident in the psalm, the perspective of the one whose reality/presence/effectiveness is under question. As the human community on earth raises the question of God, *in heaven* precisely the opposite question, the question of the human, is being raised. From this perspective the same data—humans are all alike corrupt; no one does good—calls into question not the reality of God but the character of the human. A divine judgment is being made about the whole of humankind: Is there anyone who seeks after God, that is, who hates evil, loves the good, and works for justice in the human arena? The answer is a stark No! The data, you see, cut both ways. They raise the issue of the reality of God, the theodicy question, but they also say that is the question about the human. You hear the same kind of question raised by God in Jeremiah:

> Run to and fro through the streets of Jerusalem,
>> look around and take note!
> Search its squares and see
>> if you can find one person
> who acts justly

and seeks truth—
so that I may pardon Jerusalem. (5:1)

And remember how the book of Job starts, in the heavenly assembly, with the Lord's looking down from heaven on the human (as in Ps. 14:2) and once again—as in Psalm 14 through a third voice, the Satan—raising a question about the *human* reality: Is there one who will hold to the conviction of God's presence and God's justice when the facts seem to point in another direction? (Job 1:9–11). The brief exchange between Job and his wife is instructive precisely because of its similarity to what we encounter in Psalms 10 and 14: "Then his wife said to him, 'Do you still persist in your integrity? Curse God, and die.' But he said to her, 'You speak like one of the foolish women. Shall we receive the good at the hand of God, and not receive the bad?'" (Job 2:9–10 AT). While we are sympathetic toward Job's wife, it is not an accident that Job says his wife speaks like one of the foolish ones. Here also the question about the human from the perspective of the divine is being raised alongside and right in the middle of the human question about God.

The Knowledge of God

Despite all the attention we have given it, we are not quite finished with Psalm 14. There is another large question or issue that rises within its brief text. It is the matter of the *knowledge of God*, and I mean that in both the *subjective* sense (How does God know us, and what does God know about us?) and the *objective* sense (How do we know God, and what do we know about God?). We start with the latter question: How do we know God? Let us take note of the psalmist's question in Psalm 14 after the opening assertion about the fool's thought and the reason for it. The psalmist says: "Have they no knowledge, all the evildoers who eat up my people as they eat bread, and do not call upon the Lord?" (v. 4). It is quite possible to see this as simply asserting that the evildoers do not know they will be punished. That certainly gains some support from Psalm 9:16: "The Lord has made himself known, he has executed judgment" (or better, "He has done justice" [AT]).

However, I think it is something more or other than that, not only in the sentence from Psalm 14 but what Psalm 9 says as well. I expect the psalmist refers here to the knowledge of God more generally, which seems to happen through the activity of justice and righteousness and living by God's way. The prophet Hosea spells this out the best, for the knowledge of God is one of his primary themes, and it is clear that such knowledge comes in the act of keeping the law.

> My people are destroyed for lack of knowledge;
>   because you have rejected knowledge,
>   I reject you from being a priest to me.
> And since you have forgotten the law of your God,
>   I also will forget your children." (Hos. 4:6)

Knowledge is learning and obeying the will of God with faithfulness. That is indicated in the preceding verses as the prophet says: "There is no faithfulness or loyalty, and no knowledge of God in the land" (v. 1b). How does one know that? The answer is in the next verse: "Swearing, lying, and murder, and stealing and adultery break out." Not keeping the Ten Commandments is evidence that there is no knowledge of God. The famous divine declaration in Hosea 6:6 confirms what these other texts indicate:

> For I desire steadfast love and not sacrifice,
>   the knowledge of God rather than burnt offerings.

Hosea is not the only prophet who helps us understand what the psalmist has in mind when he says "Have they no knowledge, all the evildoers who eat up my people as they eat bread?" (Ps. 14:4). Jeremiah's oracle to Jehoiakim is every bit as specific about the knowledge of God:

> Are you a king
>   because you compete in cedar?
> Did not your father eat and drink
>   and do justice and righteousness?
>   Then it was well with him.
> He judged the cause of the poor and needy;
>   then it was well.
> Is not this to know me?
>   says the LORD.
> But your eyes and heart
>   are only on your dishonest gain,
> for shedding innocent blood,
>   and for practicing oppression and violence. (Jer. 22:15–17)

And when Isaiah describes the ideal Davidic king and his way of ruling—"With righteousness he shall judge the poor"—he concludes by declaring, when that day comes, "the earth will be full of the knowledge of the LORD, as the waters cover the sea" (Isa. 11:4, 9).

What we have in all this is a rather firm conviction that among the components making up the knowledge of God and sometimes seeming to exhaust the total content of the knowledge of God—is obedience to the moral demands of God as reflected in the covenant responsibility: justice and compassion, steadfast love and faithfulness. That is how one knows God in the double sense of that term, both as acknowledgment of God and knowing who God is. The Lord of the Psalms, the Lord of Scripture, says, in effect, that "You cannot come to know me apart from the life you live with your brothers and sisters."

The *subjective* knowledge of God—God's knowledge of us, or "What does God know about us, and how does God have that knowledge?"—arises at two places in the Psalter that seem to interact with each other. The first of these, Psalm 73, once again sets us before the wicked and their questioning of the reality of God, doubting the effective power of God, in this case, to know what is going on. The psalm begins with the psalmist's envy of the arrogant and the prosperity of the wicked (v. 3) and describes this in some detail:

> They are not in trouble as others are;
>   they are not plagued like other people. (v. 5)
> They scoff and speak with malice;
>   loftily they threaten oppression.
> They set their mouths against heaven,
>   and their tongues range over the earth. (vv. 8–9)

Then the psalmist says:

> Therefore the people turn and praise them,
>   and find no fault in them [text uncertain].
> And they say, "How can God know?
>   Is there knowledge in the Most High?" (vv. 10–11)

Once again the ability of the wicked to carry out their oppressive ways with impunity raises the question of God, in this instance whether God even knows what is going on.

Quite a different perspective on God's knowledge of the human creature is given to us in Psalm 139. There the psalmist elaborates at some
length how it is impossible to escape from God and the fact that the Lord
knows everything about the supplicant:

> O LORD, you have searched me and known me.
> You know when I sit down and when I rise up;
>   you discern my thoughts from far away. (vv. 1–2)

There is nothing about the human being unknown to God. Even before
the psalmist speaks, the Lord knows everything one is going to say. And
any efforts to flee from the divine presence and knowledge are doomed
to failure, whether the supplicant flees to heaven or to hell. In fact, God
knew all about this person before birth: the Lord knew what lay before
the psalmist while still in the womb. And at the end, the psalmist is still
known to God or still with God (vv. 17–18).

This long articulation of the extent and scope of God's knowledge of
all the psalmist's ways and words and thoughts seems to stand in some
tension with the way the psalm ends. After an imprecation against all
those who are God's enemies, the psalmist says: "Search me, O God, and
know my heart; test me and *know* my thoughts. See if there is any wicked
way in me, and lead me in the way everlasting" (vv. 23–24). Why this
petition by one who has claimed there is nothing God does not know
about oneself? The dissonance, in fact, is not as strong as it seems. There
is a direct line from the first verse of the psalm to these verses. The first
verse might be more precisely translated as: "You have searched me and
come to *know* [my heart]." The initial clause is crucial. The Lord has
come to know the heart of the psalmist only after a process of searching
or testing.

Such understanding is not peculiar to this psalm but is present in other
psalms and throughout the Old Testament. There are some things God
does not know about us without some process of testing, searching, and
probing. In Psalm 66 and elsewhere, especially in the Prophets (e.g., Jer.
6:27–30; 12:3), the testing (*bḥn*) is in the context of an image of testing
and refining:

> For you, O God, have tested us;
>   you have tried/refined us as silver is tried/refined.
>   (Ps. 66:10 AT)

The matter is not just knowing where the people are but also refining to purify the people. Two other contexts function especially as settings for God's testing to know. For Israel as a whole, the critical—but not the only—period of Israel's testing is the time in the wilderness, and we hear several times of God's testing Israel there (Exod. 15:25; 16:4; 17:2; etc.). The process of testing, which seems to happen again and again, is summarized in Psalm 81:7:

> In distress you called, and I rescued you;
> > I answered you in the secret place of thunder;
> > I tested you at the waters of Meribah.

Perhaps the experience and its intention is best summarized in Deuteronomy 8:2:

> Remember the long way that the LORD your God has led you
> > these forty days in the wilderness,
> in order to humble you, testing you to know what was in your heart,
> > whether or not you would keep his commandments.

It is not a matter of general knowledge about the people that God seeks. It is to know what is in their hearts and specifically, Will they keep the commandments? There is a real question, and its answer requires the Lord's testing and searching to find out which way the people will go. This is the knowledge of us that the Lord seeks.

The other primary context in which we encounter frequent reference to God's searching and testing in order to know the heart and mind of the human creature is the laments or prayers found in the Psalms and elsewhere. God is called upon as "you who test [*bḥn*] the minds and hearts" (7:9). Psalm 11:4–5 speaks of the Lord as the one whose "gaze examines [*bḥn*] humankind," who "tests [*bḥn*] the righteous and the wicked." Then in Psalms 17 and 26, the prayer of the psalmist specifically offers himself or herself to be tested and examined by God so that the Lord may know one's righteousness:

> If you try [*bḥn*] my heart, if you visit me by night,
> > if you test [*ṣrp*] me, you will find no wickedness in me. (17:3)

> Vindicate me, O LORD, for I have walked in my integrity,
> > And I have trusted in the LORD without wavering.

Prove[*bḥn*] me, O LORD, and try [*nsh*] me;
test [*ṣrp*] my heart and mind. (Ps. 26:1–2).

The protestations of innocence on the part of those who cry out in distress is often expressed in an openness to God's test so that God may know him or her and know that she is truly innocent and righteous. The matter of God's testing to know the human heart comes up in Jeremiah's laments as well (11:20; 12:3; 20:12). And Job even raises the question as to whether the human being can fool God in the process of testing and searching: "Will it be well with you when he searches you out? Or can you deceive him, as one person deceives another?" (Job 13:9).

There is one further word that takes us far from the Psalms textually, but not in substance. The story of God's command to Abraham to sacrifice his son has perplexed and disturbed generations. How can a loving God make such a demand of a human being? For many, this is almost a line in the dirt. There are, of course, many facets to the story, but whatever our judgment about God from this story, we must be attuned to two things: One is that there is no sacrifice of Abraham's son. I would call him Isaac, but the story makes it clear that what counts is the relationship: "your son, your only son Isaac, whom you love" (Gen. 22:2). And that is one of the keys to the story. The other matter that is central to what is going on is the opening sentence, often ignored: "After these things, God tested Abraham." If we are not sure what is meant in the other texts to which I have referred when they talk about testing and searching, this story makes it clear. Everything hangs in the balance, literally the whole of human history if one takes the Bible seriously. It all depends on whether Abraham, called to be the agent of God's blessing in the world, will walk the way the Lord has set for him. Can Abraham be trusted? The preceding stories have not made that clear. So now he is put to the test, and what is crucial is that God does not know without the test. That becomes evident at the climax of the story when Abraham raises the knife and the angel of the Lord stops him, saying: "Do not lay your hand on the boy or do anything to him; *for now I know that you fear God.*" It is hard for us to believe that God does not know these things about us, but the Bible tells me so—and that God will find us out as we are tested.

The critical question of how we are known by God thus has an open door, according to the Psalms and other voices in Scripture. Divine omniscience is qualified at what may be the most crucial point: knowledge of the human heart. It is clear from these texts that God can and will come to know, but God's knowledge of us is not as open and transparent as we may think. It depends upon God's investigation, God's process of discerning and shaping, of testing and proving, to see which way we will go: in disobedience and wickedness, or in obedience and trust.

Chapter Two

God among the Gods

Although I grew up in a family deeply rooted in the Reformed tradition and constantly reading and learning the Psalms, I do not recall encountering Psalm 82 until I was in graduate school, where I was given it as an exegesis assignment. It was not like anything else I knew of in the Psalter or, for that matter, in the rest of the Old Testament. Now of course, there are connections, and I want to explore them. Yet the psalm seemed to me to be *sui generis*, and it still seems that way. Though I have written about it in other contexts,[1] I continue to be drawn to it, feeling not only its uniqueness but also its power and significance.

I am not alone in that regard. In his book *The Birth of Christianity*, the New Testament scholar John Dominic Crossan has called this psalm "the single most important text in the Christian Bible."[2] That is a large claim for any text, and quite interesting in coming from a Jesus scholar like Crossan. Whether one agrees with him or not, he manages to whet one's appetite for looking at this relatively obscure and peculiar text.

Psalm 82

[1]God has taken his place in the divine council ["council of El"];
  in the midst of the gods he holds judgment:
[2]"How long will you judge unjustly
  and show partiality to the wicked? *Selah*
[3]Give justice to the weak and the orphan;
  maintain the right of the lowly and the destitute.
[4]Rescue the weak and the needy;
  deliver them from the hand of the wicked."

[5]They have neither knowledge nor understanding,
     they walk around in darkness;
     all the foundations of the earth are shaken.

[6]I say, "You are gods,
     children [sons] of the Most High, all of you;
 [7]nevertheless, you shall die like mortals,
     and fall like any prince."

[8]Rise up, O God, judge the earth;
     for all the nations belong to you!

The One and the Many

In some respects, Psalm 82 is the closest thing we have in the Scriptures
to a truly mythological piece, a poem that is set entirely in the world of
the gods. And it is couched in a way that suggests it represents a turning point in the history of religions. That is, one cannot deal with this
text without seeing in its structure and movement a proposal for how
one is to view the divine world, the world of the gods, one that suggests
some movement there and not simply a mute and unchanging reality. Of
course, the movement may be very much a perception from the human
perspective, but certainly in this text, that movement and change take
place entirely in the divine world. Maybe one should take that seriously
and see here a mythological playing out or enactment of what has happened in the history of religions. While there is much to this psalm that
cannot be explored in a single lecture or chapter, I want to look at how
it goes about defining deity in its complexity and in its essential character. And to begin with the complexity, I am reminded of a statement by
the ethicist James Luther Adams, who said, "We live in a cosmos that is
social."[3] That is, the interaction and relationship of the one and the many
is not simply an issue in the ethics of the human but also belongs to all
of reality, including the divine world. And it does not necessarily begin
with the Trinity.

In Psalm 82, there are at least *four* perspectives discernible on the relationship between God and the gods:

1. The God of Israel, YHWH, or the LORD, is shown at the beginning of the psalm as a member of the divine council, one among the
gods. In "the council of El"—the council of the high god, El, executive

of the pantheon, well-known from the mythological literature of ancient Ugarit—the LORD, here named or called Elohim (I shall come back to that) takes his stand, that is, rises out of the divine world of which he is understood to be a part and begins to judge the gods (the elohim). Thus the psalm suggests a picture of *YHWH/Elohim as being a part of and coming out of the gods.* We hear echoes of such a perspective outside the Psalter. In the ancestral narratives of Genesis, the high god El is associated with the gods of the ancestors, the God of Abraham, Isaac, and Jacob; in Exodus we hear God tell Moses, "I am the LORD. I appeared to Abraham, Isaac, and Jacob as [El Shaddai,] God Almighty, but by my name 'The LORD [YHWH]' I did not make myself known to them" (Exod. 6:2–3). It is quite possible if not likely that in some fashion YHWH is a split off from El. It is not surprising, therefore, that the El names and epithets are appropriated and acceptable in Israel's religion. That is where YHWH comes from.

2. If, however, as Psalm 82 suggests, the LORD comes out of the world of the gods, it is also the case that YHWH shares with the gods of the nations common functions and responsibilities. In the process of this court scene, YHWH takes over the divine world and its responsibilities so that what belonged to the gods now becomes solely vested in YHWH, the LORD. The psalm also suggests—or we may infer—a relationship in which *the gods and their character are in YHWH.* Taking over the divine realm involves appropriating the aspects and responsibilities of all the gods. There is an interesting intimation of this within the language of the psalm. The Tetragrammaton, the divine name (*yod he waw he*, יהוה), does not appear anywhere in the psalm, where the divine name is given as *ʾĕlōhîm* (vv. 1, 8), as is the case often in the Old Testament. That feature can be handled literarily by observing that Psalm 82 belongs to what is called the Elohistic Psalter, a group of psalms that show a preference for the word *ʾĕlōhîm* over the Tetragrammaton when referring to the God of Israel (Pss. 42–83). In this particular psalm, however, the Elohim name does more. One becomes aware of the ambiguity of the term, how it can be a proper name, "Elohim," or a common noun, "gods," either singular in referring to the God of Israel, as it does twice in the psalm, or plural in referring to all the other gods, as it also does twice in Psalm 82. By using the word "elohim" in these ways, the psalm reminds us that the term is always capable of pointing to something more or other. It is a literary way of reminding us that the gods are in YHWH, and YHWH is part of the elohim.

Confirmation of this absorption of other deities or their characteristics is evident in the Psalms and elsewhere. A classic example is the presentation of the Lord as the storm-god in Psalm 29:

> The voice of the LORD is over the waters;
>> the God of glory thunders,
>> the LORD, over mighty waters. (v.3)

Long ago H. L. Ginsberg argued that this psalm is a Canaanite hymn to Baal, the only change being the replacement of the name "Baal" with the Tetragrammaton, a point that finds its confirmation when the replacement is reversed and the three consonants of the Hebrew name Baal are reinserted.[4] Then one will find heavy repetition and wordplay with those three consonants throughout the whole psalm, clearly suggesting the likelihood that the original divine figure of the psalm was Baal, whose character as the god of the storm has been fully absorbed into YHWH.[5] But one does not encounter YHWH in the Old Testament as one particular kind of deity, god of storm, mountain deity, personal god, warrior god, and so forth. There is not a peculiar character to this deity. The possibilities are too numerous, for there are few if any aspects of the cosmos and its rule and governance that are not explicitly associated with YHWH.

3. What is most obvious in Psalm 82 is the *confrontation and conflict between the LORD—YHWH/Elohim—and the gods*, which ends with his condemning them to death as he assumes sole rule, *the LORD against the gods*. While the critical term for "gods" is debatable at the beginning of Psalm 58, that psalm seems to reflect the kind of judicial metaphor for the conflict between YHWH and the gods that we have in Psalm 82. It begins:

> Do you indeed decree what is right, you gods?
>> Do you judge people fairly?
> No, in your hearts you devise wrongs;
>> your hands deal out violence on earth. (58:1–2)

Then the psalm proceeds to describe the actions of the wicked:

> The wicked go astray from the womb;
>> they err from their birth, speaking lies.

They have venom like the venom of a serpent,
  like the deaf adder that stops its ear.... (vv. 3–4)

If the opening reference is to the gods, as seems likely, then we have much the same thing going on in Psalm 58 as in Psalm 82, an indictment of the gods for their failure to stop the wicked from carrying out their evil deeds. We should note in passing that this judicial metaphor is prominent in Deutero-Isaiah as the LORD summons the gods into the courtroom in order to demonstrate their inability to act as gods in declaring and bringing about what is to happen. The outcome is the disappearance of the gods as a delusion (Isa. 41:21–29).

4. The relationship between God and the gods, however, is not finally one of conflict. As Psalm 82 comes to an end, there is at least an implicit claim that *the LORD will rule over the gods of the nations*, a dominance manifest and reflected in a righteous rule of the earth and attested elsewhere in the Psalms, particularly in that climactic group of Psalms that declare "the LORD reigns" over all, the Enthronement Psalms of Book IV (Pss. 93 and 95–99). Assertions of the LORD's reign over the gods are not confined to the Enthronement Psalms, however. As Book III of the Psalter comes to an end in Psalm 89, the question is asked: "Who among the heavenly beings is like the LORD?" (v. 6) and immediately answered: "God feared in the council of the holy ones, great and awesome above all that are around him" (v. 7). Such a claim, echoed in Psalm 29, "Ascribe to the LORD, you divine ones, ascribe to the LORD glory and strength" (AT), makes it clear that the gods have been turned into worshipers of the Lord; the occupants of both heaven and earth bow down before the maker of earth.

Psalm 82 suggests to us, therefore, a way of viewing the reality of God that is open to complexity and differentiation, to continuity and discontinuity, while also claiming and insisting on unity and order. Nowhere in the rest of Scripture do we get so clear a picture of the divine council as a sociopolitical order suggesting complexity in the divine world while also insisting on the one rule of the one God as shaping and directing it. The divine assembly continues to be a significant feature of Israel's religious conviction and of the Scriptures that portray it. So in the creation narratives and later in Genesis, divine commands are several times in the plural: "Let us make . . ." and "Let us go down and . . ." (1:26; 11:7). When Isaiah is called, the Lord on the throne, surrounded by the seraphim, says: "Whom shall I send, and who will go for us?" (Isa. 6:8).

And in Micaiah's vision of the heavenly assembly, there is discussion and planning that takes place among the participants (1 Kgs. 22:19–23). The condemnation of the gods to mortality does not mean the end of the complexity of divinity; the cosmos is still social.

Defining Deity

The Living God

Out of this complex and sociopolitical world as one sees it in Psalm 82 come two critical matters in regard to defining and distinguishing the God who takes over from the other gods. One aspect of that distinction is *the difference between the living God and the dying gods.* The mortality of the other gods joins with what the Psalms and other texts say about idols and images. The latter have no power. They are, as Psalm 115 and other psalms put it, "the work of human hands" (v. 4). "They have mouths, but do not speak; eyes, but do not see" (v. 5). They are powerless. Over against this is the claim of Psalm 82 and the rest of Scripture that God lives. Several things need to be observed about that claim:

1. The notion that God is dead or may be dead is not an invention of modern philosophy or a passé theological movement of the 1960s. It was one of the liveliest issues in the ancient world.

2. The conception of God as living is a part of general characterization of deity in the ancient Near East. The expression we hear in Psalm 18:46, "The LORD lives!," corresponds to the jubilation cry in Ugaritic/Canaanite myth, "Baal lives," after the earlier cry "Baal is dead." Related to this is language about God's *sleeping.* In a mythological context, God's resurrection was God's "awaking." The Psalms take over this kind of language to call for effective power from the Lord. The call to God to awake is frequent in the Psalms. So in Psalm 44:23:

> Rouse yourself! Why do you sleep, O Lord?
> Awake, do not cast us off forever!

In two instances, the call to the Lord to awake is in order to bring about justice. Psalm 7:6, "Awake, O my God; you have appointed a judgment [or commanded justice]"; and Psalm 35:23, "Wake up! Bestir yourself for my defense [*mišpāṭ*], for my cause, my God and my Lord!" In this context sleep is a picture for the attitude of the *Deus absconditis*, of God who is silent and does not intervene, who has not yet evidenced life and power to the oppressed. Because sleep was the time when the divine power was broken and ineffective, the psalmist in one of the most beloved of all Psalms claims:

> The one who keeps you will not slumber.
> Behold the one who keeps Israel
>   will neither slumber nor sleep. (Ps. 121:3–4 AT)

3. The language "God lives" or "the LORD lives!," which we find in Psalm 18:46, occurs most often in the oath "As the LORD lives," a usage that points to God as witness and judge (e.g., Ruth 3:13). It places the most serious matters under the confession and conviction of the living God, that is, the claim that nothing of weight matters or happens except out of the reality that God is living, dynamic, capable, effecting everything. It is, in a sense, an acknowledgment of the truth of the mythological claim that when God dies, everything else dies. To say "God lives" or "as God lives" when we say something is also a testimony to the seriousness and truthfulness of what one says, a willingness to place one's words and being under the watchful and powerful presence of a living God, knowing with the author of Hebrews that "it is a fearful thing to fall into the hands of the living God" (Heb. 10:31).

4. With this notion of the living God, several things are claimed or inferred: (a) What is living is more than a memory. The living God means a present reality. (b) Whatever is living is not subject to our control. (c) Whatever is living makes demands on us. And (d) to speak of God as living is to count God as involved with the rest of life. Here appears the notion, so central to the Psalms, of God's responsiveness to the human situation: God has passion and compassion, suffering and pain. The rule and power of God are never broken. They may be hidden. Clearly, as we see all through the Psalms, Israel wrestled with the problem of *Deus absconditus*. But it was for Israel *Deus absconditus*, God hidden, not *Deus mortuus*, god dead, as it was for Baal.

And according to Psalm 82, so it was for the whole divine world. In the ancient world, gods died and even came back to life. Something rather different, however, happens in Psalm 82. For this is not the story of the death of a god; it is a judgment against the whole divine realm that condemns it to mortality, to death, so that the power and effectiveness of the gods is no longer possible. They are like human beings. The living God has condemned the gods to death. Their power is gone.

Justice for the Poor

Perhaps the most important word of the psalm, however, and the definitive answer it gives to how one defines deity is found in the reason why
the gods are condemned to mortality. It is anything but obscure. Indeed,
the point is underscored by repetitive speech in a way that few texts,
ancient or contemporary, demonstrate so clearly. The most obvious of
the repeated words is the verb *šāpāṭ*, "to judge, to do justice," occurring four times in the psalm; once at the beginning and once at the end
with regard to the work of the God who takes over in this psalm. That
is, God's speech against the gods, Elohim's death sentence pronounced
on the gods, is an act of judgment and justice. So also at the end of the
psalm, the future work of God and the hope of all the earth is for God
to enact justice for and upon all nations. In marked distinction from this
strong identity of Elohim with the enactment of justice is what we hear
about the rest of the gods. Again the word for justice and judgment is
used twice, once in Elohim's query to the council of the gods: "How long
will you judge unjustly?" with its counterpart in the next verse: "Give
justice to the weak and the orphan; maintain the right of the lowly and
the destitute" (vv. 2–3).

And with these verses we encounter the other large category of repetitive speech, *five different terms (with one repeated) for the weak and the poor*.
While it is not possible to differentiate sharply among the terms, they all
have to do with the weak, the needy, and the poor; some of them more
precise, as in reference to the orphan. The other terms, however, are all
capable of identifying members of the community who are impoverished,
weak, and/or needy in some fundamental way, specifically, in need of
material and/or legal assistance:

> Give justice to the weak and the orphan;
>> maintain the right of the lowly and the destitute.
> Rescue the weak and the needy;
>> deliver them from the hand of the wicked. (vv. 3–4)

It is difficult to imagine a more explicit way of defining what is missing in the divine world, what role defines deity in a life-or-death way. It
is the provision of justice for the weak and the poor when what is happening is injustice and preferential treatment for "the wicked," the term
in the Psalter that, from the first verse onward, is the all-encompassing
term to describe the rich and powerful who oppress the weak and the

poor. Psalm 1 begins, "Blessed is the one who walks not in the way of the wicked" (AT), and Psalm 82 says this is the very fundamental issue on which the world hangs. The rule of the cosmos is oriented toward the wicked, which means injustice toward the weak and the poor. The destiny of the gods, of the rule of the universe, now hangs on this one thing: justice for the poor. There is no catalog of divine sins, no internal conflict in the divine council. It is all reduced to a single issue. Even when the text goes on to speak of the gods as having "neither knowledge nor understanding" (v. 5), that is a reference to their maladministration of justice, as we know from Deuteronomy, where those who are to be chosen as judges should be persons who are "wise, discerning/understanding, and knowing" (Deut. 1:13 AT).[6]

And it is not just the fate of the gods that is at stake. The fate of the universe is at risk in the face of the rulers' failure to rule justly, as we hear at the end of verse 5: "All the foundations of the earth are shaken." When justice for the weak does not happen in the divine world, the outcome is literally earthshaking: the world disruption and deities dying; the one an outcome, the other a permanent effect.

Now while this psalm is so unique and unusual, even as it is so direct and explicit, I want to show how it resonates with so much of the rest of the Psalter. To some extent all that happens in the Psalter is accounted for in this Psalm. It may not be in any technical, literal, or redactional sense the center of the Psalter, but it is the foundation on which most of it rests. Let me give three examples to illustrate:

1. The largest single group of psalm types is the genre of lament, essentially a prayer for help. It is precisely the outcry of the weak and the poor, the powerless and the needy, who live in a world where the wicked, referred to over eighty times in the Psalms, are often shown partiality. The legal codes of the Bible refer to the outcry and God's listening specifically with regard to the orphan and the widow (Exod. 22:21–24) and the poor and needy (Deut. 15:9; 24:14–15). One may and should assume that while we often do not have any clear or specific way of defining the one who prays such a prayer as these lament psalms, the voice is that of the poor, the weak and the needy, the orphan and the widow—all of whom cry out for justice, as at the beginning of Psalm 86: "Incline your ear, O Lord, and answer me, for I am poor and needy"; and whose voice is heard and answered, as seen in Psalm 9:12: "He does not forget the cry of the afflicted." Their cry is for justice (Ps. 7:8, "Judge me, O Lord, according to my righteousness"), to be rescued and delivered, to be saved from the oppression of the wicked (Ps. 9:9, "The Lord is a stronghold for

the oppressed"). What the gods have not done, according to Psalm 82, and what Elohim has called for (v. 1) and is called to (v. 8)—that is what most of these prayers are about.

2. In similar fashion, one of the primary themes of the Psalter, present in both the lament prayers and in the songs of thanksgiving and praise, is that the Lord is the one who will judge and deal justly. From Psalm 7 with its claim that "God is a righteous judge" (v. 11) to Psalm 113's depiction of the Lord who "raises the poor from the dust and lifts the needy from the ash heap" (v. 7), the justice and compassion of God for the weak and the poor is central to the theology of the Psalter, to its portrayal of the Lord of the Psalms. Nowhere is this view of Elohim/YHWH more pronounced than in the group of Psalms 93 through 99, commonly called Enthronement Psalms because of their declaration that the Lord is King, a theme that some have argued provides the theological center of the Psalms.[7] More than any other group, these psalms declare the exaltation of the LORD/Elohim above all the gods: "For the LORD is a great God, and a great King above all gods" (95:3). "For great is the LORD, and greatly to be praised; he is to be revered above all gods" (96:4–5). "All gods bow down before him"(97:7). Elohim's takeover of the divine world, that glimpse into the divine world that Psalm 82 gives us, is now the presupposition of all the psalms and to which they all bear witness. The Lord is king, and the rule of this king is just and compassionate. That is attested from the beginning (Pss. 2; 9:7–8, 16–18) to the end (Ps. 146:7–10) but is especially the climactic declaration of the Psalter in the Enthronement Psalms. There we hear echoes of the last verse of Psalm 82: "Rise up, O God, judge the earth." Amid the Enthronement Psalms, the psalmist in Psalm 94 asks: "Who rises up for me against the wicked?" (v. 16). Psalms 96 and 98 conclude and climax with the declaration "For he is coming to judge the earth. He will judge the world with righteousness and the peoples with equity" (Pss. 96:13; 98:9), in both cases making this expectancy follow upon the announcement that the Lord is King. Psalm 99 makes the definitive claim "Mighty King, lover of justice, you have established equity; you have executed justice and righteousness in Jacob" (v. 4); and Psalm 97 reminds us that "righteousness and justice are the foundation of his throne" (v. 2). None of this is confined to these psalms, however. Thus in Psalm 76:8–9 we hear: "From the heavens you uttered judgment; the earth feared and was still when God rose up to establish judgment, to save all the oppressed of the earth."

Perhaps the climactic echo of Psalm 82 is the word we hear in response to the announcement in Psalm 82:5 that because the gods do not know or understand and walk in darkness, the foundations of the earth are shaken. Now we hear twice, in Psalm 93 and 96, that the Lord is King; he has established the world, and *it shall never be shaken*. The endangerment of the universe by the absence of justice in the world is overcome by the just rule of the Lord. The prophets call for justice in the land. The Psalms tell us the *world* hangs by that thread, that the godness of God depends upon the execution of justice to deliver the weak and the poor. No wonder the Lord says, "My wrath will burn," when the abused widow and orphan "cry out to me" (Exod. 22:24). God's own reputation, God's own divinity, depends on what happens when that cry goes up.

3. The third reflection of the new world after Psalm 82 and the reinforcement of its definition of deity is the role of the king as we find it in the (royal) Psalms. The rule of the human king is the preeminent *imitatio Dei*, as reflected in broad terms in a psalm such as Psalm 101, which begins with "I will sing of *ḥesed* and *mišpāt*, of steadfast love and justice" and ends with the declaration "Morning by morning I will destroy all the wicked in the land." The clearest and most explicit presentation of the rule of the king as an imitation of the rule of the Deity is Psalm 72. It begins with the call "Give the king your justice, O God, and your righteousness to a king's son. May he judge your people with righteousness, *and your poor with justice. . . . May he defend the cause of the poor of the people, give deliverance to the needy, and crush the oppressor*" (vv. 1–4). Then the psalm goes on at length with prayers of blessing upon the king: "May he live while the sun endures. . . . May he have dominion from sea to sea. . . . May all kings bow down before him, all nations give him service" (vv. 5–11). Why should such enduring, rich, and universal rule be the outcome for this king? Verses 12–13 are very explicit about that: "*Because* [AT] he delivers the needy when they call, the poor and those who have no helper. He has pity on the weak and the needy, and saves the lives of the needy." The rationale for all the blessings before and after these verses is the king's just rule in behalf of the poor and the needy. What defines divine rule defines human rule. Further, the prosperity and flourishing of human society depends solely upon this one factor: maintenance of justice to save the weak and the poor.

So it is that in Psalm 82 a significant and unprecedented theological step is taken: the death of all the gods. Its whole basis is the moral behavior of the human community, more particularly the presence or absence of justice as defined by what happens to the weak, the powerless, the poor members of society, or one might say, how the systems of order provide for the right of such persons. And that is not simply a matter for the human realm. The very claim to deity rests upon the question of whether or not the gods have carried out such moral supervision, ensuring the presence of justice in the human communities for which they are responsible.

And in a sense the point of the psalm, by its *story* or *narrative* character, is that henceforth Israel is to view the world as directed by a single moral purpose, reflected in the God that it has come to know in its experience. There are not ultimate powers at work in competition with each other or ruling in different spheres. There is only one Lord of the universe, and the claim to be the only one rests upon this God's insistence on a justice-shaped universe. Psalm 82 is a story, literally, of how the divine world was forced into radical change in the face of human injustice and oppression of the poor. On that day the gods died because they did not sustain a world where justice and deliverance for the weak and the needy could be maintained. Christian faith and Judaism have lived ever since that day with the moral burden of monotheism. It is there in every theodicy issue, and Psalm 82 says God wants to be judged precisely on these grounds, as it concludes: "Rise up, O God, judge the earth." Maybe this *is* the most important text in the Bible. If not, it may be the most disturbing.

Chapter Three

The Body of God

God-Talk in the Psalms

When our son Jonathan was about three or four years old, and not long after we had made a trip overseas that included an overly eventful and extended stay in the airport at Paris, trying to keep Jonathan occupied while we waited many hours for plane repairs, Mary Ann was tucking him in bed one evening and saying a bedtime prayer with him. Shortly after they finished the prayer, I was about to enter the room to give him a good-night kiss when I heard him ask his mother, "What does God look like?" I came to a quick halt and stood silently in the hall, thinking, "I believe I'll let Mary Ann handle that question." She did so very capably, I thought, saying something like this: "We don't really know what God looks like, but we know what Jesus was like, and that tells us something about what God is like." And then she began to elaborate that. I was impressed with this quick and theologically perceptive response to the child's question. But during the third sentence into her elaboration, Jonathan looked up at her with sleepy eyes and said, "Oh, Mom, just tell me about Paris."

The question "What does God look like?" seems indeed a childish question and the answer seems obviously what Mary Ann said: "We don't know what God looks like." But I wonder if our rejection of the question is entirely appropriate. At least at one level, it seems to be somewhat premature when one stops to consider how much attention is given in the Bible to what God is like. Depictions of God in various ways abound in Scripture. And while one may quickly and easily say that we are not to take them literally, there are still questions: How are we to take such depictions? What are we to make of them?

In other words, we cannot read the Psalms or any part of Scripture without being confronted with portrayals of God. As others have observed, one of the most striking features of biblical language is its anthropomorphisms. In the Bible, preference is given to particular and concrete modes of speech over abstract modes, and personal modes are favored over impersonal ones. That does not mean that other modes are excluded (e.g., "I am holy," "God is love," "I am the truth"), but priority is given to the particular and the personal, and even the more abstract is framed within the particular and the personal. That this is the case should not be surprising. If one should seek cultural or phenomenological reasons for the preference or use of this language, there would seem to be at least two:

1. This is the mode of linguistic perception possible and appropriate to the people involved (Israel and its neighbors).
2. It reflects the nature of what is being talked about: a history or story of a people's way in the world in encounter with and relationship with a God who sets and directs that way.

This last point is especially acute, for it has much to do with how we speak of God. The character of Scripture presses upon us a view of God or ways of speaking about God that belong to the story character of Scripture and its subject matter and to its thematic focus on God's involvement in the world and with a people from the beginning to the end. In other words, the mode of speech is not simply a choice but a given.

Before exploring some of the more personalistic language with which the Psalms speak of God, let me make an observation. Generally we take for granted the modes of speech about God that we encounter in Scripture and to some extent take them for granted in our own usage. But that is a little too simple. This language, the biblical mode of speech about God, can quickly become an issue if not indeed a problem. Let us illustrate:

1. For many people, anthropomorphic language is a problem. God is not a person; such a way of speaking is limiting, even silly at times, such as seeing God's back (Exod. 33:23), God's walking in the garden (Gen. 3:8), and the like.
2. Theological language, the language of systematic theology, fairly quickly finds it necessary to shift to more abstract, reflective language, such as speaking of God as the ground of being (so Tillich),

the center of meaning and value (H. Richard Niebuhr), the Princi-
ple of Concretion or the ground of concrete actuality (Whitehead),
or the dynamic acting reality beyond Limit (Gordon Kaufman).
3. In our time the issue has been sharply raised by the feminist resistance to the standard modes of personalistic language of the Bible
and the tradition in using male language and metaphors to speak
of God.

Scripture generally, however, and certainly the Psalms, does not let us
flee from the more anthropomorphic speech about God.

The very question "What does God look like?" naive and childish
though it may have been when our son uttered it, is in fact very revealing. Both conceptuality and connection, understanding and relationship, seem to demand some way of *encountering* or *conceiving*—and we
may speak of it both ways—God as embodied and personal. We are, of
course, not accustomed to thinking or speaking of God as embodied, as
having body, until we get to the New Testament, but the notion of incarnation only makes sense in the New Testament if it reflects, points to, or
arises out of what we know about God in the Old Testament. There are
extensive references to bodily dimensions of the Deity in the Psalms. One
may dismiss them as metaphorical, and indeed they are. But it is also the
case that apart from these bodily dimensions, we do not know the God of
Scripture. Even with regard to the third person of the Trinity, the Holy
Spirit, we encounter the Spirit within ourselves, as that which animates
us, so that it is not finally possible to speak of even the Spirit as non-
personal and apart from bodily connections. Indeed, the Psalms parallel
God's spirit with God's face: "Where can I go from your spirit? Or where
can I flee from your presence [face]?" (Ps. 139:7). Whichever person of
the Trinity we may have in mind at any point, we always speak of persons. And persons are known to us only by their presence and action and
emotion—how they appear and act and feel and communicate. There is
a tendency to assume that the wide use of metaphorical or analogical language with reference to God means that the personal/anthropomorphic
material is only metaphorical and not literal. Perhaps it is not a matter
of deciding between metaphorical and literal so much as it is recognizing
the *necessity* of the personal and embodied God-talk, which then suggests
that it may also be truthful.

That such is the case for the Psalms is evident in a variety of ways.
Let me illustrate five areas or categories where the analogical or metaphorical language of the Psalms confronts us with God embodied and

personalized. In each instance we also encounter representations that stand in tension with such ways of imaging or perceiving—and again we may speak of these representations in both ways, reckoning such speech as originating in our own minds or as something that is given to us.[1] The five categories of God-talk are these:

- body
- name
- voice and speech
- space and place
- temporality

Body Language for God

Among the bodily features most prominent in the Psalms is the *"face"* of God. As Leong Seow has noted, the word "face," *pānîm*, often means simply yet importantly "personal presence."[2] He also observes that the language signifying "the most direct personal encounter," "face-to-face," occurs several times but only in the encounter of "human beings with the numinous." Thus Jacob wrestles with a stranger and names the place Peniel, "face of God" because "I have seen God face to face" (Gen. 32:30). The Lord speaks to Moses "face to face, as one speaks to a friend" (Exod. 33:11).[3] Let me mention three ways the face of God is spoken of with some frequency in the Psalms. One is the face as object of a verb, such as "seek" or "see" or "come before." An example is in Psalm 105:4: "Seek the LORD and his strength; seek his face continually." As Seow observes, such a way of speaking in other contemporary cultures meant to visit with another or to come and see the king or the cult image of the deity.[4] The face refers to a person or some embodiment of personality in an individual, a monarch, or a cult image.

One may not too quickly reduce such language to metaphor if such reduction eliminates what is meant by the image: *direct and personal encounter*. To seek the Lord or come before the Lord often has specific reference to the sanctuary, as in Psalm 42:2, which begins, "When shall I come and behold the face of God?" (v. 2), and ends in Psalm 43 with the good news and expectation "Let them bring me to your holy hill and to your dwelling" (v. 3). The concreteness of the language, the intensity and specificity of the face, prohibits a choice between literal and metaphorical. The encounter with God is personal, local, real. In the Psalms, to see or seek or come before God's face is most likely an entry into the place where the ark rested, the divine throne. While our focus on the aniconic in ancient Israel leads us to emphasize the invisibility, someone is there, enthroned on the cherubim. We tend to focus more on the invisibility than the reality of God's personal presence. The *language of face* is a constant reminder that what is sought, what fills with joy (Pss. 16:11; 21:6), what merits praise, is an encounter with the person of the Divine.

A fairly frequent reference to the face of God in the Psalms is found in a number of laments that complain that God has hidden God's face. The reasons are not specific enough to know what the cause is, but the expression clearly has to do with the experience of separation from God, God's absence from the life and fate of the psalmist. In most instances the reference to the hidden face is in a plea: "Do not hide your face from me" (Pss. 27:9; 69:17; 102:2; 143:7), do not abandon me in my plight; or in a complaining question: "Why do you hide your face from me?" (Pss. 44:24; 88:14). God's face being hidden means that God is not involved and not paying attention to what is going on. If the face of God is a primary expression of the personal presence of God, with all the positive possibilities that means, the hidden face of God is just the opposite. Such circumstance is a terrifying situation for the psalmist.

The third idiom involving the face of God is a reflection of the Aaronic benediction, whose blessing is heavily weighted toward the effects of God's face or countenance: "The LORD bless you and keep you; the LORD make his face to shine upon you, and be gracious to you; the LORD lift up his countenance [face] upon you and give you peace" (Num. 6:24–26). Several times in the Psalms we hear pleas for such blessing: "Let the light of your face shine on us, O LORD!" (4:6). "May God . . . make his face to shine upon us" (67:1). "Let your face shine, that we may be saved" (80:3, 7, 19). Here is the most substantial clue to what belongs to the face of God: shining light. The phenomenology is not specific, but surely it has to be the presence of light in the darkness, or light against the darkness. The key term is "light"; however it is experienced, it is an aspect of the reality and person of God. Thus Psalm 27 begins: "The LORD is my light and my salvation," and 36:9 reinforces the point with the psalmist's claim: "In your light we see light." Psalm 104 speaks of God as wrapped in light, which is also the beginning of creation. The letter of 1 John says it very simply: "God is light and in him there is no darkness at all" (1:5).

We are accustomed to thinking of the announcement in John's Gospel of Christ's coming into the world in terms of the Word, but the dominant language of that preface is of light: "What has come into being in him was life, and the life was the light of all people. The light shines in the darkness, and the darkness did not overcome it. . . . The true light, which enlightens everyone, was coming into the world" (John 1:3–5, 9). Later Jesus himself will say, "I am the light of the world" (8:12). Saul's conversion in Acts 9 is a dramatic encounter with a light from heaven and a voice speaking. When Saul asks, "Who are you, Lord?" the answer comes, "I am Jesus, whom you are persecuting" (Acts 9:3–5). Paul heaps up the language of light and its concreteness in the face of Jesus Christ when he writes: "For it is the God who said, 'Let light shine out of darkness,' who has shone in our hearts to give the light of the knowledge of the glory of God in the face of Jesus Christ" (2 Cor. 4:6). This in effect is saying that the shining of God's face is now in the shining of the face of Jesus Christ, a confirmation of Mary Ann's answer to Jonathan's question, "What does God look like?"

The body language in the God language of the Psalms is not confined to face. Not infrequently one will encounter the face language alongside hand and arm, as in Ps. 44:3:

> For not by their own sword did they win the land,
>   nor did their own arm give them victory;
> but your right hand, and your arm,
>   and the light of your countenance,
>   for you delighted in them.

Or in reference to the eyes and ears of God, as in Psalm 34:15–16:

> The eyes of the LORD are on the righteous,
>   and his ears are open to their cry.
> The face of the LORD is against evildoers,
>   to cut off the remembrance of them from the earth.

The language of God's eyes and ears is especially important for the psalmists and for any assumption that prayer is an authentic act with legitimate expectations. "Incline your ear to me" or "Give ear to my cry" is among the most common petitions of the Psalms. That does not mean that the matter of God's "hearing" could not be contested. The presumption of the righteous or the innocent is that there are ears. The presumption of the wicked is that there are not. As Psalm 94 puts it:

> They kill the widow and the stranger,
>   they murder the orphan,

and they say, "The LORD does not see;
the God of Jacob does not perceive." (vv. 6–7)

To which the psalmist responds:

Understand, O dullest of the people;
fools, when will you be wise?
He who planted the ear, does he not hear?
He who formed the eye, does he not see? (vv. 8–9)

The argument is rational; the conclusion means everything. If there
are no ears and no eyes, then the one to whom the pleas are raised cannot hear the cry or see what is wrong. The assumption that there is some
reflection of the reality and embodiment of God in the human creature
is the ground for all our praying. The biblical story is one of human pain
and suffering. It begins with and is carried by the capacity of God's ears
to hear the cry of the oppressed, whether it is Abel's blood crying from
the ground (Gen. 4:10) or the outcry against Sodom that comes up to
God (Gen. 18:20). The story of redemption in the exodus begins with
the words of the Lord: "I have seen the misery of my people who are in
Egypt; I have heard their cry on account of their taskmasters. Indeed, I
know their sufferings, and I have come down to deliver them from the
Egyptians" (Exod. 3:7–8a). The Lord repeats this claim in the next verse:
"The cry of the Israelites has now come to me; I have also seen how the
Egyptians oppress them" (v. 9).

In at least two ways it is evident that the widespread characteristic of
the Psalms to speak of God in body language does not exhaust our God-
talk or limit our capacity to think and speak about God really. One way
is in the experience of encounter with the divine that one finds in Psalm
139. There the body language is very present but articulated in a way that
lifts up God's pervasive presence:

Where can I go from your spirit?
Or where can I flee from your presence [face]?[5]
If I ascend to heaven, you are there;
if I make my bed in Sheol, you are there.
If I take the wings of the morning
and settle at the farthest limits of the sea,
even there your hand shall lead me,
and your right hand shall hold me fast. (vv. 7–10)

It is easy to read this as leading to the simple conclusion that God is everywhere. Nor can one fault that reading. It is part of the way the Psalms preclude our appropriating the body language in a limiting fashion. Yet the focus here is on the psalmist, and the point is that God is everywhere *with me*. One may seek God's face in the sanctuary, but God's face is always there. One may experience suffering as God's hiding of "your face," but as the psalmist in that paradigmatic prayer of Psalm 22 discovers and declares, "He did not hide his face from me, but heard when I cried to him" (v. 24b).

That body language does not exhaust our God-talk is evident in the Psalms, especially in the propensity for this poetically theological speech to draw on all sorts of metaphors and images to express something of God's way and walk, of God's presence and power, some expressions as engaging or capturing as any of the embodiment language. One has only to think of the simple statement "The LORD is my shepherd," clearly nonliteral speech but pointing to a crucial reality that can hardly be described in any other way and still be highly personal (Ps. 23:1). Both in Psalm 23 and elsewhere, the psalms elaborate on that image because it so describes how one should—and wants to—understand the relationship between the Lord and me, the Lord and us, "the sheep of his pasture" (Ps. 100:3). Sometimes such images overlap with human experience so that the role or image is carried by both God and the human persons, as in Psalm 127:1

> Unless the LORD builds the house,
>   those who build it labor in vain.
> Unless the LORD guards the city,
>   the guard keeps watch in vain.

The overlap of divine and human activity, of divine and human roles, is a poetic reminder once again of the inseparability of the reality of the human and the reality of God. As I was writing this sentence, my NYTimes browser flashed up a headline to the effect that physicists at the Fermi National Accelerator Laboratory had uncovered clues to explain human existence. It was too complicated for me to follow except that it had to do with why there is more matter than antimatter, which is why there is a universe—from a scientific perspective. What caught my attention was the final sentence of the article, quoting Joe Lykken, a theorist at the Fermi Lab: "So I would not say that this announcement is the equivalent of seeing the face of God, but it might turn out to be the toe of God."[6]

There are of course, other powerful and theologically crucial personal images of the Lord of the Psalms, such as king and judge and warrior, a triad of images that are at the center and heart of the Psalter.[7] Equally important for the God language of the Psalter is the way in which those who pray these prayers draw on nonhuman images to express some of the most important convictions about our encounter with God, as in the opening of Psalm 18:

> I love you, O Lord, my strength.
> The Lord is my rock, my fortress, and my deliverer,
>   my God, my rock in whom I take refuge,
>   my shield, and the horn of my salvation, my stronghold. (vv. 1–2)

Or similarly in Psalm 91:

> You who live in the shelter of the Most High,
>   who abide in the shadow of the Almighty,
> will say to the Lord, "My refuge and my fortress;
>   my God in whom I trust."
> . . . .
> He will cover you with his pinions,
>   and under his wings you will find refuge. (vv. 1–2, 4)

Yet we recognize that the personal language does not disappear with such images. A good friend once spoke of my father as a rock and my mother as an eagle. Those images spoke powerfully about their personalities, their ways of being and doing, and their relationships with other persons.

The robust body and personal language of the Psalter is echoed or present elsewhere in the Old Testament but also stands in a kind of tension with expressions that seem to resist or delimit the embodiment of God. One thinks of the divine assertion in Hosea 11: "I am God and not a human being, the Holy One in your midst" (v. 9 AT). Or Moses' words in Deuteronomy 4: "Then the Lord spoke to you out of the fire. You heard the sound of words but saw no form [*tĕmûnâ*]; there was only a voice" (v. 12). In contrast to this stands Psalm 17, which speaks throughout its verses of the ears and eyes and lips of God, the hand and right hand, and then concludes with these words: "As for me, I shall behold your face

in righteousness; when I awake I shall be satisfied, beholding your likeness [form, *tĕmûnâ*]" (v.15). In Deuteronomy, no form is seen; in Psalm
17, both face and form are seen. What we must not miss in this tension,
however, is that in Hosea the divine contrast between God and human
being occurs in a context of some of the most extensive presentation of
the divine reality in highly anthropomorphic and personal language to be
found anywhere: "I took them up in my arms. . . . I led them with cords
of human kindness. . . . I bent down to them and fed them" (Hos. 11:3–4).
In Deuteronomy 4, Moses' words are clearly tied to the danger of formful
images made by human hands, violating the First and Second Commandments: "Since you saw no form [*tĕmûnâ*] when the LORD spoke to you at
Horeb, . . . take care . . . that you do not act corruptly by making an idol
for yourselves in the form [*tĕmûnâ*] of any figure—the likeness of male
or female" (vv. 15–16). In the Psalter, seeing the face and form is access
to the Deity and encounter with the holy that is the desire of covenantal
existence. In speaking to and about God, we live with both the reticence
of Deuteronomy 4 and the boldness of Psalm 17.

God's Name

The personhood of God is made explicit also in the *divine name*. While we
are accustomed to thinking of the book of Exodus (3:13–15) with regard
to the name of God—for there we have the revelation of the name of
God in Moses' encounter with the LORD—in the Psalter there are about
a hundred references to the "name" of God along with all the actual uses
of the name. Sometimes reference to "the name" is in poetic parallelism
to a reference to God or a citation of the name, as in Psalm 44: "Through
you we push down our foes; through *your name* we tread down our assail-
ants" (v. 5). "In *God* we have boasted continually, and we will give thanks
to *your name* forever" (v. 8). Often they are together, as in "Sing praise to
the *name* of the LORD, Most High" (Ps. 7:17). So reference to "the/your
name" is a substitute for the actual name itself, but it is more than that.
The name alludes to the character and reputation of the one who bears
it: "And those who know your name put their trust in you" (9:10). "Your
name, O LORD, endures forever, your renown, O LORD, throughout all
ages" (135:13).

A number of times, the plea goes up for God to act "for your name's
sake." This name is associated with acting in such a way, and so the reputation and validity of the personality bearing the name is at stake in how

that one acts.[8] Names bear a particular weight and point to a manner of being. They serve to distinguish persons from one another. Having a name is central to personal identity and uncovers not only the persona or character but also the reality of the one so named. It is as critical as the personal embodiment language for knowing, encountering, and experiencing the reality of God, manifest in power, protection, and glory. In Psalm 22, the psalmist hears and receives God's answer to the extended prayer for help and then declares:

> I will tell of your name to my brothers and sisters;
>> in the midst of the congregation I will praise you. (v. 22).

The name encompasses who and what God is and is like. So it is important not only that God has a name but also that the name as such is acclaimed. To invoke the name is both to identify oneself with the name bearer and to call upon the reality that bears the name to be and act according to the character and reputation of that one. Knowing the name means knowing what this one is like. Thus the psalmist says:

> And those who know your name put their trust in you,
>> for you, O Lord, have not forsaken those who seek you. (9:10)

It matters immensely that this one has a name, for only so can this one be called upon, identified, understood, and praised.

Alongside the name that is revealed in the story of the exodus and carried through in the Psalms and elsewhere as the Tetragrammaton, usually represented by the term "the Lord [יהוה, YHWH]," there is also another term that is both name and not quite name: "Elohim." Here the name is also a category: "god" or "gods" or "the God." As it is applied to the same one who is called "the Lord" or can substitute for the divine name, it becomes clear that the personal name of God exhausts the category of deity. They are one and the same thing.

God's Voice and Speech

To speak of a personal God means not only one who is presented in *embodied language* and *bears a name*. It also involves one who can and does *communicate*. Speech and voice, word and language—these are also parts of what it means to be person. One is inclined to think of the Psalms as primarily the voice of human beings' addressing God, which is why there is so much reference to the face of God and the ears of God. In fact, however, there are a number of places where God speaks in the Psalms. Indeed, there are indications that what the psalmist seeks and wants from God as much as help and deliverance is a word, a spoken assurance. We hear that in Psalm 35 when the one praying says:

> Contend, O Lord, with those who contend with me;
> . . . .
> Draw the spear and javelin
>   against my pursuers;
> say to my soul,
> "I am your salvation." (vv. 1, 3)

The psalmist clearly seeks divine action but also seeks a word from the Lord that is a profound assurance, one that changes everything. A lament prayer in Lamentations gives us another picture, this time remembering the experience of God's response:

> I called on your name, O Lord,
>   from the depths of the pit;
> you heard my plea,
>   "Do not close your ear to my cry for help,
>   but give me relief!"
> You came near when I called on you;
>   you said, "Do not fear!" (3:55–57).

In yet another form, the psalmist anticipates the speech of God to the people:

> Let me hear what God the Lord will speak,
>   for he will speak peace to his people. (85:8)

Just such words as these—"Do not be afraid," "I am your salvation," "I am with you," "Peace be upon you"—not only are the speech of God; they also are transforming speech. One of our best clues to that is the psalm that comes after the model lament prayer of Scripture, Psalm 22, the psalm that becomes the interpretive key to the meaning of Christ's passion in the Gospels. The turning point of the psalm in 22:21 is the psalmist's exclamation: "You have answered me" (AT, Masoretic Text). The extended prayer of thanksgiving that follows this answer to the psalmist's terrible suffering (22:22–31) is then followed immediately by the psalm of trust that we know best with its words:

> Even though I walk through the darkest valley,
>   I fear no evil;
> for you are with me;
>   your rod and your staff—
>   they comfort me. (23:4).

The one praying needs not only to be heard but also responded to. The speech of God turns night into day, death into life. Such words of assurance are as crucial to the reality and persona of the Divine as the cries are to the reality and persona of the human.

Yet in the Psalms it is also evident that this voice so speaking is not simply the same as any other voice. In Psalm 18:13 we read:

> The LORD also thundered in the heavens,
>   and the Most High uttered his voice,
>   hailstones and coals of fire. (AT)

The same point is made in unparalleled way in Psalm 29:

> The voice of the LORD is over the waters
> . . . .
> The voice of the LORD is powerful;
>   the voice of the LORD is full of majesty.
> The voice of the LORD breaks the cedars . . . of Lebanon.
> . . . .
> The voice of the LORD flashes forth flames of fire.
>   The voice of the LORD shakes the wilderness;
> . . . .
> The voice of the LORD causes the oaks to whirl. (vv. 3–9)

This voice that speaks and responds, that communicates and assures—this voice is also a voice that shapes and controls nature, that creates and sustains as well as comforts, something we have learned from the very beginning of the biblical story.

God in Relation to Space and Time

The Psalms also tell us that the Lord of the Psalms is to be understood in personal and embodied thought and language because the Lord is *somewhere*. That is, as every human being exists in some real space and has a place, so it is that the one whose face is sought is understood to be available in particular places. God has a location, a place where God resides. Indeed, the Lord has multiple locations. The Psalms speak of them often.

One of the most extended references to God's dwelling or place of habitation is Psalm 132, where the people say:

> "Let us go to his dwelling place;
>   let us worship at his footstool." (v. 7)

This is then complemented by the Lord's own words:

> For the LORD has chosen Zion;
>   he has desired it for his habitation:
> "This is my resting place forever;
>   here I will reside, for I have desired it." (vv. 13–14)

And in numerous other places we hear of God's dwelling place in Zion (74:2; 76:2), or God's shining forth out of Zion (50:2). Similar are the references to the Lord's being in his temple (11:4), hearing the cry of the psalmist from his temple (18:6), and beholding the beauty of the Lord in his temple (27:4). Often there is simply a reference to "the house of the LORD/God" (e.g., 23:6; 27:4; 42:4; 52:8; etc.) or "your house" (e.g., 5:7; 65:4; 66:13; 84:4; 93:5). There is one explicit reference to the ark (132:8) but other probable references (e.g., 80:1; 99:1).

While I have referred to multiple locations, all of these references assume a single location—the house of the Lord. God has a home, a place to meet and be met, a place where the Lord may be found. As Karl Barth has put it succinctly: "In the Old Testament testimony and the Old Testament form of the revelation, there is always a dwelling place of God which can be marked on the map."[9] That there is mobility is important, of course, and that is found in the ark (and elsewhere in the tabernacle). Both place and movement are dimensions of the living God as they are of living persons. In this case, as it may be in human experience, the dwelling place of God is shared by others (e.g., Pss. 23:6; 27:4).

With equal vigor and frequency, the Psalms affirm the *heavens* as God's space. And here is where the poetry of the Psalms enables the community to hear and comprehend poetically what elsewhere requires more theological analysis and argument. I am thinking of Solomon's long dedicatory prayer with its frequent petitions of the following sort:

> But will God indeed dwell on the earth?
>> Even heaven and the highest heaven cannot contain you,
>> much less this house that I have built!
> Regard your servant's prayer and his plea, O Lord my God,
>> heeding the cry and the prayer that your servant prays to you
>>> today;
> that your eyes may be open night and day toward this house,
>> the place of which you said,
>> "My name shall be there,"
> that you may heed the prayer
>> that your servant prays toward this place.
> Hear the plea of your servant and of your people Israel
>> when they pray toward this place;
> O hear in heaven your dwelling place;
>> heed and forgive. (1 Kgs. 8:27–30)

Without reference to the name as being in the temple and God's dwelling place as in heaven, Psalm 11 simply says: "The Lord is in his holy temple; the Lord's throne is in heaven" (v. 4). The Lord is present in both places. There is no effort to explain such dual dwelling. But God's place in human space, clearly spelled out in so many ways, can only be apprehended alongside the place outside human space. The psalmist who says, "From his temple he heard my voice" will go on to say "He reached down from on high, he took me" (18:6, 16). Whenever the throne of God is specifically located, it is in the heavens (103:19). A number of times we hear of God's sitting or dwelling in the heavens (e.g., 2:4; 33:14; 123:1). And countering all of this, we also hear that God, who created the heavens in which the Lord is enthroned, is over or *above* the heavens: "You have set your glory above the heavens" (8:1). "Be exalted, O God, above the heavens" (57:5).

> The Lord is high above all nations,
>> and his glory above the heavens.

Who is like the LORD our God,
  who is seated on high,
who looks far down
  on the heavens and the earth. (113:4–6)

"Where is God?" we often ask. Well, God is in different places,
according to the Psalms: in the Lord's house located in Zion, and in the
heavens, and wherever I am. But these heavens were made by the Lord,
and the God who dwells on earth in the temple and is enthroned in the
heavens also is indeed above and beyond the heavens. What is clear is that
one cannot simply take one of these locations or the other. The point is
not a universal dwelling, but the Lord with us and beyond us: both spaces
are absolutely crucial to how we are known and kept by God and how we
know and encounter God.[10]

God and Temporality

Finally, one must ask about *temporality* and its presence or absence in the
reality that is God. The sharp difference between God and human beings
in this regard is present in Psalm 90 as it begins its extended reflection
on human temporality and mortality, the short span of our life, with a
confident claim:

LORD, you have been our dwelling place
  in all generations.
Before the mountains were brought forth,
  or ever you had formed the earth and the world,
  from everlasting to everlasting you are God. (vv. 1–2)

Whatever may be our limited life, there is no limit on God's life. The
point is reinforced in Psalm 102, where sharp contrasts are made between
God's eternity and the finitude and limit of all creation. Like Psalm 90,
this is done in the acute awareness of our human mortality:

"O my God," I say, "do not take me away
  at the midpoint of my life,
you whose years endure
  throughout all generations." (102:24)

Then the point is elaborated as the psalm comes to an end:

> Long ago you laid the foundation of the earth,
>   and the heavens are the work of your hands.
> They will perish, but you endure;
>   they will all wear out like a garment.
> You change them like clothing, and they pass away;
>   but you are the same, and your years have no end. (vv. 25–27)

This marked difference between human beings and God is a great benefit. We perish, but God endures and is the same always.

That this contrast is a benefit is evident particularly in how the point about God's being everlasting or from everlasting to everlasting (Ps. 90:2) is most often made—not with God as the subject but with God's rule (e.g., 9:7; 10:16; 66:7; 93:2; 145:13) or God's steadfast love (103:17; cf. 100:5; 106:1; 107:1; etc.) as everlasting. What the eternity of God means is that God's love for us is always available. Psalm 90 makes its point that God is from everlasting to everlasting. Indeed, there is no end to God, but the point about divine eternity has to do most often with us. That is, God's time is our time, and what distinguishes God from us relative to temporality and eternity is the perdurance of the experience of God's love and faithfulness as well as God's rule of this finite world. And when Psalm 102 says with reference to God, "You are the same, and your years have no end" (v. 27), the point is not so much something about the being of God as it is the hope of the human, as the following and final verse makes clear:

> The children of your servants shall live secure;
>   their offspring shall be established in your presence. (v. 28)

While God's eternity may be categorically different from our temporality, it is at the same time the ground for the security of human temporality that God's love and faithfulness shall never end because God never ends and God's rule is for all of time.

In all of this I hope you see that whether it is our intention or not, whether we wish to go forward or not, it is finally impossible to close our eyes and ears, our hearts and minds, to the resonances of all of this with the revelation of God in Jesus Christ. Indeed, I would argue that all we have been talking about is preparation and the way to the incarnate Word: the incarnation is the outcome of all that we have seen here. The embodied person of God is real, even as that embodiment does not exhaust the fullness of deity. Jesus experiences human finitude and mortality, but that is not the last word (Phil. 2:6–11). The spoken word of God is revealed in Jesus, the Word that became flesh and dwelled among us. And we have seen his glory. The name of this one is Emmanuel, "God is with us," and Jesus, "He will save us," the name at which every knee shall bow. The revelation of God in Jesus Christ is the Yea and Amen to all that the Psalms tell us of the person of God in and with us, seen and seeing, named and naming, speaking and listening, here and there, now and forever.

Chapter Four

Maker of Heaven and Earth

The first article of the Apostles' Creed defines God the Father Almighty in a concise and simple way: "Maker of heaven and earth."[1] In so doing, it appropriates one of the familiar and repeated descriptions of the Lord of the Psalms (115:15; 121:2; 124:8; 134:3; 146:6). As a kind of epithet, this description is a presumption and a ground for all sorts of other things that are said or claimed about the Lord, some of which we shall explore. There is only one psalm, however, that focuses entirely upon the creative work of God: Psalm 104. As the primary elaboration of God's creative activity, it commands our attention.

God as Maker of All

That Psalm 104 is a self-conscious elaboration of the basic claim "Maker of heaven and earth" is evident from the start. The psalm begins with the reality of God: "You are very great. You are clothed with honor and majesty, wrapped in light as with a garment" (vv. 1b–2a). The description of God in terms of greatness, honor, majesty, and light is offered not simply as a list of divine attributes but also as the Lord's clothing, which leads into a description of God's abode and mode of transportation. In so doing, the text immediately launches into a presentation of God's *creation of the heavens*: "You stretch out the heavens like a tent, you set the beams of your chambers on the waters, you make the clouds your chariot, you ride on the wings of the wind" (vv. 2b–3). God's greatness and majesty are manifest in the creation of the heavens. God's character and being are intimately tied into what God has wrought: the wonder of the heavens. There is a marked interdependence between God and the heavens,

47

underscored in the words of Psalm 115:16: "The heavens are the LORD's heavens."

But creation of the heavens is not apart from creation of the earth, and the psalmist slides directly into that aspect of the making of heaven and earth: "You set the earth on its foundations, so that it shall never be shaken. You cover it with the deep as with a garment;" (vv. 5–6a). What is noticeable as one keeps reading is that there is a continuous creation of earth going on, and once again this shows a marked interdependence but of a different sort. If "The heavens are the LORD's heavens," according to Psalm 115, one must acknowledge with the psalmist that "the earth he has given to human beings" (115:16b). There are two realms that interact but are markedly distinguishable. And as there is an interdependence but distinguishability between God and the heavens, the same is true of earth and its inhabitants.

Psalm 104, however, makes or sees things with more complexity than does Psalm 115. For in this psalm we encounter a community of nature, of living beings, both animal and human. There is no exaltation of the human creature, no ruling dominance. Human beings do not even get into the picture until after extensive description of animals and birds and God's creative work to provide for them, both place and food and water. When they first appear, it is only as a parallel to cattle as recipients of God's provision of food (v. 14). The second appearance of *ʾādām* (human[s]), once again, is alongside the animals of the forest, who come out to get their food at night and return to their dens in the daytime, when human beings go out to work and labor until evening (vv. 19–23). The interdependence of heaven and earth is manifest in the way in which the moon marks the seasons and the sun determines day and night (vv.19–23), a point that is made precisely to show the difference between the active time of the animals and that of human beings. The latter do not show up again as a separate category until we get to the end of the psalm and its words about sinners and the wicked (v. 35). Meanwhile, the young lions are roaring, the birds are singing, and Leviathan is playing in the great waters of the sea. Creation is God's ongoing and unending activity, and the world is complex and full of creatures human and otherwise. Psalm 104 is as much about water and trees and goats and wine and bread as it is about the place of human beings in God's created order. Their place is identified but always alongside the other creatures, animals and birds, "living things both small and great" (v. 25).

From the perspective of the whole, the creation—particularly the earth, which is the primary focus of the psalm—is sure, reliable, and satisfying.

Its purposefulness is everywhere manifest (e.g., vv. 10–12, 14–23). Its beauty is evident in the positive depiction of the trees and vegetation and animals. Creation—heaven and earth and all that is therein—is not just there. Psalm 104 is a theological grounding of the large claim of Genesis 1 that heaven and earth, everything that God had made, is good, indeed *very good*. In Genesis 1 this point is underscored as the evaluating judgment of the Creator. In Psalm 104, the goodness of creation is elaborated from beginning to end. The outcome is joy in the creation (vv. 15, 31, 34) and praise of the Creator (vv. 1, 24, 33–35). Before the Psalter is over, all of heaven and earth shall join in praise of the Maker of heaven and earth (Psalm 148).

Although Psalm 8 does not celebrate and praise the Creator as much as Psalm 104 does, the Lord's creative work is very much its subject matter. Psalm 8 is a psalm of praise, but what evokes that praise is the wonder of God's creation and especially as that is manifest in the human creature. Even here, however, it is only after the recognition of God's power and glory in the creation of the heavens that the psalmist then stops and thinks about how incredible it is that God has given such a place to a mere human being:

> When I look at your heavens, the work of your fingers,
> the moon and the stars that you have established;
> what are human beings that you are mindful of them,
> mortals that you care for them? (vv. 3–4)

The power of this psalm is in its way of expressing awe at the created order such that it seems to make nothing of human beings, but all of that on the way to the highest anthropology in the pages of Scripture:

> Yet you have made them a little lower than God [or: the divine beings].
> and crowned them with glory and honor.
> You have given them dominion over the works of your hands;
> you have put all things under their feet,
> all sheep and oxen,
> and also the beasts of the field,
> the birds of the air, and the fish of the sea,
> whatever passes along the paths of the seas. (vv. 5–8)

In contrast to Psalm 104, the human being is not simply one of the creatures God has made. The human has been given rule over the creation, over God's handiwork. Psalm 8 thus presents us with an interpretation or elaboration of what Psalm 115 means when it says, "The earth he has given to human beings" (v. 16).[2] It would be difficult to imagine a higher view of the place of human beings in the divine cosmos. The human creature is here described in royal and divine terms, setting humanity on high in every way possible and placing all that is on earth under human rule and care:

> Ps. 115 makes the same point in a slightly different way: "The heavens are the LORD's heavens, but the earth he has given to human beings" (v. 16). It is a religious and theological claim that "You" have given human beings dominion over the works of "your hands," that human rule of the natural order is a divinely given vocation. It is also a part of general human experience that being human means turning nature into culture, seeking to tend to, control, and use the natural order.[3]

What is not to be missed in either Psalm 8 or Psalm 104 is the ultimate aim of all that is said about the making of heaven and earth. Psalm 8 begins and ends with the exclamation: "O LORD, our Sovereign, how majestic is your name in all the earth," and Psalm 104 begins and ends with "Bless the LORD, O my soul" and climaxes with the sudden interrupting exclamation, "O LORD, how manifold are your works!" (v. 24a): thus we are aware that all this talk of creation, and in very different terms, is entirely "to the praise of his glory" (Eph. 1:12, 14). Psalm 148 rings the changes on this cacophony of praise as it describes a chorus of praise encompassing all of creation: "Let them praise the name of the LORD, for he commanded and they were created" (v. 5).

That Psalms 8 and 104 give us very different pictures of the created order relative to the role of the human creature in it does not mean we are to choose one of these pictures over the other. It is quite crucial that both depictions are included in the Psalter, for both of them speak truthfully, wisely, and pedagogically about the place of the human in God's created order. Genesis 1, our primary creation story, sets the creation of human beings at the end of the story and as a piece of the large picture of creation of light and darkness, heaven and earth, waters and seas, fertile plants and trees with fruit, stars, moons, and planets, creatures of all sorts in the waters and in the air and on the ground. Finally human beings are created in God's own image. In one sense they are simply part of the whole, as in Psalm 104, the culmination of a created

universe. But as we learn also from Psalm 8, this creature among creatures has a special role to play, an assigned rule over the created order.
Then at the end of the creation story and the announcement of the ruling assignment given to the human animal, God announces a provision
of food and in so doing makes that provision as basic for all the animals
as it is for human beings:

> God said,
> "See, I have given you every plant yielding seed
>   that is upon the face of all the earth,
>   and every tree with seed in its fruit;
>   you shall have them for food.
> And to every beast of the earth,
>   and to every bird of the air,
>   and to everything that creeps on the earth,
>   everything that has the breath of life,
>   I have given every green plant for food."
> And it was so. (Gen. 1:29–30)

Thus the story of creation in Genesis 1 conjoins what we hear in both
Psalm 8 and Psalm 104. There is a marvelous universe that God has created and a world of nature that is full of animals and food in various
forms. Among the animals is the human being, a creature who also is
given dominion and rule over the other animals. Thus the reader of the
Psalms is invited to see in the making of heaven and earth the creation of
a world of creatures who have their particular places, their particular food
patterns, their different ways of functioning in the natural world—yet
also a particular relationship in which one of the creatures is given a ruling assignment vis-à-vis the others. In many respects, however, they live
in God's creation in similar ways, as is underscored in the verses quoted
above from Genesis 1 and in Psalm 104:14–23, which tell of God's provision of food for all the creatures, not just the human being.

What is very clear from Psalm 104 is that there is little distinction
between creation and providence in that God's creative work continues
in the provision of water and grass and food and plants (cf. Ps. 65:9–11).
Creation is a continuing activity even as it is clear that heaven and earth
were made long ago (cf. Ps. 102:25). Psalm 104 seems to present a seamless continuity between the origin of heaven and light, clouds and winds,
and the daily provision of plants and food, of bread and wine. Indeed,
what we see here is what we see as we look at the world of which we are a

part. Nothing is truly still and finished. The universe goes on in countless ways. In contrast to Genesis 1:1–2:4a and its word about God's finishing "the work that he had done" and resting (2:2), the maker of heaven and earth, as praised in Psalm 104, has never ceased this creative work, even if much was done in the past. The contrast between these texts, however, is an accurate reflection of the way human beings and other creatures experience the heavens and the earth that God made. There are all sorts of evidence of what was done long ago. There is a sense of the completion of creation. The only new creation is eschatological, a fulfillment and perfection of what was begun at the beginning. But we are also well aware that from the very first moments of the creation of the universe, as we know it, from the Big Bang onward, the making of heaven and earth has been a continuing, ongoing reality or action. Each day continues what the Lord began in the making of heaven and earth.

One of the psalms that particularly sets forth a recounting of God's creative work and then identifies all the ways God fills the earth with richness—water, grain, and food—is Psalm 65. In brief fashion, the psalmist seems to draw on the ancient depictions of creation as subduing the waters of chaos:

> By your strength you established the mountains;
>   you are girded with might.
> You silence the roaring of the seas,
>   the roaring of their waves,
>   the tumult of the peoples.
> Those who live at earth's farthest bounds are awed by your signs;
>   you make the gateways of the morning and the evening shout
>   for joy. (65:6–8)

Then the psalm pictures God's provision for the needs of the earth:

> You visit the earth and water it,
>   you greatly enrich it;
> the river of God is full of water;
>   you provide the people with grain,
>   for so you have prepared it.
> You water its furrows abundantly,
>   settling its ridges,
> softening it with showers,
>   and blessing its growth.

You crown the year with your bounty [goodness];
    your wagon tracks overflow with richness. (vv. 9–11)

Then, as in Psalm 104 and Psalm 8 as well as Psalm 148, all of this leads to the praise of God. Psalms 65 and 148 explicitly describe the praise rendered by the richly endowed natural world:

The pastures of the wilderness overflow,
    the hills gird themselves with joy,
the meadows clothe themselves with flocks,
    the valleys deck themselves with grain,
    they shout and sing together for joy. (65:12–13)

Nature personified becomes an exultant choir, and the creation is a world of joy because of the rich provision of the Lord. When Psalm 150 concludes the Psalter with the call "Let everything that breathes praise the Lord!," we need to remember that other psalms incorporate the whole of creation into this choir of unending praise. All that God has made gives praise to its Maker. Perhaps that is what goes on in the bird songs that are so ubiquitous and constant—and joyous to our ears (cf. Ps. 104:12).

God as Ruler of All

The designation "Maker of heaven and earth" is a general expression and identifies a kind of action but not the actor. In contrast, the Psalms never refer to the "maker of heaven and earth" without identifying that actor as "the Lord," the one who, according to the rest of the story, delivered the Israelites from Egyptian slavery and became their God:

May you be blessed by the Lord,
    who made heaven and earth. (115:15)
My help comes from the Lord,
    who made heaven and earth. (121:2)
Our help is in the name of the Lord,
    who made heaven and earth. (124:8)
May the Lord, maker of heaven and earth,
    bless you from Zion. (134:3)
Happy are those . . . whose hope is in the Lord their God,
    who made heaven and earth. . . . (146:5–6)

Creation of the universe in its macrocosmic and microcosmic aspects is not some happenstance or the work of some distant and inaccessible and unknowable force. That may be one side of the coin, but it is not the one that lands in the Psalms. The maker of heaven and earth is the one to whom all prayers are lifted in hope and confidence, the one who is praised for the creation and by the creation, the God who is named and may be called upon.

While the Psalms repeatedly affirm that the LORD is the one who created heaven and earth, they go even further to insist that the maker of heaven and earth is also Lord of the world made by the LORD. That is, the one who made this world now rules it:

> The earth is the LORD's and all that is in it,
>   the world and those who live in it;
> for he has founded it on the seas,
>   and established it on the rivers. (Ps. 24:1–2)

It is no accident that Psalm 24 ends with one of the most extended celebrations of the Lord's kingship, for according to the Psalms, creation implies kingship and rule. These may be different aspects of the divine activity, but they are coordinate and dependent upon each other.

> The LORD is king, he is robed in majesty;
>   the LORD is robed, he is girded with strength.
> He has established the world; it shall never be moved;
>   your throne is established from of old;
>   you are from everlasting. (Ps. 93:1–2)

Or in Psalm 95:3–5:

> For the LORD is a great God,
>   and a great King above all gods.
> In his hand are the depths of the earth;
>   the heights of the mountains are his also.
> The sea is his, for he made it,
>   and the dry land, which his hands have formed.

Creation of this universe involves its rule: the two are commensurate. Clearly there is a sense of ownership, but more important is the inherent responsibility and assumption of proper rule of the world by the one who makes it. Both creation and kingship as divine aspects can arise out of conflicts and defeat of chaotic elements, but the rule of this world by the Lord is intrinsic to the fact of the Lord's having created it. And indeed that rule is found in everything from the provision of the ongoing dimensions of nature to the provision of justice for the weak and the poor (cf., e.g., Ps. 148 and below).

This last point is a matter of some significance. All too often theological discussion of creation and of God as creator, as maker of heaven and earth, stands as a separate aspect of our theology apart from other equally significant dimensions.[4] Such compartmentalization is contrary to what one finds throughout the Psalms. In the instances cited above where the Psalms speak of God as maker of heaven and earth, we notice that such description is set in the context of a claim of God's blessing or God's help (115:15; 121:2; 124:8; 134:3; 146:5–6). That is, the assertion of the Lord's creative power is regularly made in relation to expectation of God's helpful involvement with those whom God has created.

In a number of Psalms we find reference to or praise of God's creative activity alongside or intimately associated with the Lord's salvific work and the maintenance of justice in the universe. The provision of life and for life and the maintenance of continuity that is God's ongoing activity is not simply a natural phenomenon or apart from all that God does to help and provide for life, not only in the sense of food and water and sustenance but also in regard to support, protection, help, maintenance of justice, and deliverance from trouble. For example, Psalm 33, which is a call to praise the Lord, climaxes in the claim that the Lord who is enthroned in the heavens is Lord of the earth and all its inhabitants (vv. 13–19). But the ground of the multiple calls to praise is twofold at the beginning of the psalm. First, it is rooted in God's love of justice and righteousness, steadfast love and faithfulness, all of which fill the earth (vv. 4–5). And the second ground follows immediately upon the first:

> By the word of the LORD the heavens were made,
>   and all their host by the breath of his mouth.
> He gathered the waters of the sea as in a bottle;
>   he put the deeps in storehouses.
> Let all the earth fear the LORD;
>   let all the inhabitants of the world stand in awe of him.
> For he spoke, and it came to be;
>   he commanded, and it stood firm. (33:6–9)

The works of the Lord that elicit praise are simultaneously justice and creation. In this light it is not surprising that Psalm 82 defines deity in terms of the maintenance of justice. Even as the Psalms so often set that definition in terms of the power of creation, they also know that the providence of God is found in the securing of justice and righteousness. A powerful instance of this is in Psalm 146, again a psalm whose intent is to evoke the praise of the Lord who made heaven and earth. That is asserted explicitly in verses 5–6a:

> Happy are those whose help is the God of Jacob,
>   whose hope is in the Lord their God,
> who made heaven and earth,
>   the sea, and all that is in them; . . .

But before the sentence is even finished, the psalmist characterizes the maker of heaven and earth as one

> who keeps faith forever;
>   who executes justice for the oppressed;
>   who gives food to the hungry. (146:6b–7a).

And that exclamation simply opens the door as the psalmist keeps going:

> The Lord sets the prisoners free;
>   the Lord opens the eyes of the blind.
> The Lord lifts up those who are bowed down;
>   the Lord loves the righteous.
> The Lord watches over the strangers;
>   he upholds the orphan and the widow,
>   but the way of the wicked he brings to ruin. (146:7b–9)

The final word then is an assertion of the rule of the Lord—"The Lord will reign forever" (v. 10a)—which can only evoke the response "Hallelujah!" (v. 10b NJPS).

Similarly, in Psalm 147 a song of praise that focuses especially upon the Lord's provision of an ongoing natural world—rain, food, snow, hail, and wind—begins with a threefold characterization of the Lord:

- the one who builds up Jerusalem and gathers the outcasts of Israel (v. 2a)

- the one who heals the brokenhearted and binds up their wounds (v. 3)
- the one who determines the numbers of the stars and gives names to all of them (v. 4)

This three-part description encapsulates the fundamental aspects of the work and power of the Lord: (1) particular attention to Jerusalem, God's dwelling place, and the people Israel; (2) a more general concern and attention to the weak and brokenhearted; and (3) a powerful rule over the Lord's creation that never ends. The power that provides an ordered and ongoing universe attends to the weakest of those who inhabit it.

This point is carried further with the praise of the Lord as the one who "lifts up the downtrodden" (v. 6), but the psalm moves back and forth in its exultation as the reader hears echoes of Psalm 104 in the verses that follow:

> He covers the heavens with clouds,
>> prepares rain for the earth,
>> makes grass grow on the hills.
> He gives to the animals their food,
>> and to the young ravens when they cry. (147:8–9)

The final strophe of the psalm emphasizes the word of the Lord in two ways. In resonance with Genesis 1, it is the Lord's word or command that creates and provides:

> He sends out his command to the earth;
>> his word runs swiftly.
> He gives snow like wool;
>> he scatters frost like ashes.
> . . . .
> He sends out his word, and melts them;
>> he makes his wind blow, and the waters flow.
>> (147:15–16, 18; cf. 33:6–9; 148:5, 8)

But then that same word is manifest also in the statutes and ordinances given to the people of Israel:

> He declares his word to Jacob,
>> his statutes and ordinances to Israel. (147:19)

One can hardly overlook the way in which the psalm lifts up the "word" of the Lord as the creating, teaching, and ultimately redeeming mode of God's being and activity (cf. Ps. 33:6). It is one of the foundational and unifying categories for divine action as we learn of it in Scripture. The Psalms are as clear about that as are Genesis 1 and John 1.

In Psalm 65, the "God of our salvation" is praised as "the hope of all . . . the earth" (v. 5), and in the immediately following verses we hear:

> By your strength you established the mountains;
>   you are girded with might.
> You silence the roaring of the seas,
>   the roaring of their waves,
>   the tumult of the peoples. (65:6–7)

Psalm 136 begins its praise of God with an elaboration of the works of creation—the heavens and the earth, the great lights, the sun and moon and stars—and without any break or transition the psalm immediately calls for praise and thanksgiving for the Lord's bringing Israel out of Egypt, through the Red Sea and the wilderness, and into the land of their heritage. The story of creation and redemption is one story.

The communal lament of Psalm 74 grounds its expectations for God's help in the affirmation of "God my King," who works "salvation in [all] the earth" (v. 12). The psalm continues with descriptions of God as the one who "divided the sea by your might" (Is this salvation or creation or one and the same?), "broke the heads of the dragons in the waters," "crushed the heads of Leviathan," "established the luminaries and the sun," "made summer and winter," and so forth (74:13–17)—all of this being an indissoluble whole, manifesting the rule and power of God in countless ways.

To cite one more example, the prayer for help that is Psalm 102 makes its shift from the long petition-complaint of verses 1–11 into an even more extended expression of confidence and praise in verses 12–28.[5] The turning point happens in the exclamation: "But you, O LORD, are enthroned forever" (v. 12), a claim of God's ruling power reinforced with the words "The nations will fear the name of the LORD, and all the kings of the earth your glory" (v. 15). The psalm goes on to praise the Lord who heard "the groans of the prisoners" and "set free those who were doomed to die" (v. 20), yet remembers also that "long ago you laid the foundation of the earth, and the heavens are the work of your hands" (v. 25).

The inextricable conjoining of redemption and creation is nowhere more obvious and explicit than in the psalms that follow. Psalms 103 and 104 are intentionally held together by two features: the absence of any superscription between the two psalms and the presence of the same beginning and closing sentence in both psalms—"Bless the LORD, O my soul"—a sentence that occurs nowhere else in the Old Testament. This pairing brings together two of the most extensive hymns in praise of the Lord, first for the Lord's gracious and compassionate forgiveness and redemption (Ps. 103), and then for the powerful and wonderful acts of creation (Ps. 104). The two psalms are a kind of mini-theology, lifting up both redemption and creation as the ground for extravagant praise of the Lord.[6] Not to be missed is the climax of Psalm 103—and the avenue into Psalm 104—in the words: "The LORD has established his throne in the heavens, and his kingdom rules over all" (103:19). The maker of heaven and earth, the one who forgives and heals and redeems, is the ruler of all.

In the Psalms we therefore hear a powerful testimony to the work of God in creation, an activity that does not end and places the human creature as one of all God's creations but also as one who is given a role to play in God's rule of the whole creation. And if it is the case, as it seems to be, that the creative power of God never ceases and God's providential care is a part of the never-ending making of heaven and earth, then it is not surprising that the many ways in which the Lord takes care of this creation, in its various forms, incorporate the compassionate deliverance of the weak and the bowed down, the slave and the poor. To praise God as "the maker of heaven and earth" is in one sense to say it all, but only as one lets the whole story unfold.

Chapter Five

"To Glorify Your Name"

In his *Old Testament Theology*, Gerhard von Rad took up the Psalms in the context of his central focus on the theology of Israel's historical traditions; he thereby suggested that the Psalms represent Israel's *response* to the work of God as proclaimed in the saving history from Abraham to Joshua and the divine choice of David and his throne.[1] Israel's response, Israel's *answer* to the hearing of the marvelous deeds of the Lord, is to be found in the Psalms and especially in the hymns. He rightly saw both that the whole of the Psalter can be understood as human praise of the God who has created and delivered and that such praise in some sense defines the human, gives our reason for being. In the English-speaking world, such a view has been strongly emphasized within the Reformed tradition, with the most known and remembered catechetical question coming first in the Westminster Shorter Catechism, "What is man's chief end?," with its answer, "to glorify God and enjoy him forever."[2]

Von Rad was surely on the right track with his recognition that the praises of Israel as found in the Psalms are the biblical articulation of how human beings are to express the glory of God and the joy of God's presence. He did not try to confine the whole of Israel's response to the Psalter, and he recognized that there are dimensions of the Psalter that respond in another way, giving voice to the trials and sufferings of Israel as a community and as individuals within it. In this essay I want to build upon von Rad's work and carry it forward in a modest way.

Whose Initiative in the Psalms?

I begin by suggesting that seeing the Psalms theologically as the human *response* to the Deity, as Israel's *answer* to the Lord, is certainly correct but also too exclusive or narrow a picture of the place of the Psalms in Scripture and in Israel's faith. To speak of the Psalms as Israel's response is to presume that the *initiative* is entirely God's, that is, the word or deed of God to which Israel now responds. Thereby a kind of dialogue is effected. What is missing from this interpretation is the fact that in the dialogue, the initiative is often taken by the *human* member of the conversation, either in the voice of individuals or by the community as a whole. That surely happens in the prayers of the Psalter, the cries for help by persons in various kinds of trouble. Those psalmic prayers for help, however, are simply the form and voice of Israel as it cries out to the Lord again and again in the biblical story, a point that is made explicit by the attribution of psalms to David—the representative Israelite—often in particular situations of distress. They presume the existing relationship between God and the one praying, but the activity of God is often, if not primarily, initiated by the prior word of the human prayers.[3] The divine-human encounter does not always begin by divine initiative. Again and again that initiative is in response to the human cries and what they present. Thus the Psalms offer themselves as the voice of the human in the world. In this sense, as many have recognized, the Psalms contribute to the anthropology of Scripture, to its view of the human.[4] That happens, however—and this is the second thing I wish to emphasize—as a *part of what we hear about God*, the one to whom the prayers are directed.

In the various elements of the prayer for help, one learns much about the God who is the subject of the Old Testament as a whole. The exodus deliverance arises out of the crying out of the people (Exod. 2:23–25; 3:7–10). In other words, the saving activity of God as first and definitively experienced by Israel rises out of the prayer of the people. No prayer is quoted at that point, though their crying out is referred to by the Deity three times in Exodus 2–3. To comprehend what it is that moves the Lord to a saving and definitively saving act, one must turn to texts such as are in the Psalms, even if one cannot put any particular psalm as expressive of the exodus cry of the people.

In this context one cannot be exhaustive but may call to mind some of what these psalmic prayers bear witness to as characteristic of the God to whom they pray. For example:

• The God of Israel may be *trusted*, clearly one of the primary expressed and implicit assumptions of the Psalms. Elsewhere the biblical story may have much to do with whether and to what degree the *human being* can be trusted. The Psalms place their focus on the reliability of *God*, a reliability that is manifest precisely in the cries for help, described as acts of trust (Ps. 22:4–5). So the imagery for God that runs through the Psalms centers often in refuge, fortress, rock, and the like (as in Ps. 31).[5] And the prayers often express the psalmist's confidence in the delivery of help, which may only be anticipated in the psalm.[6]

• The Lord to whom these prayers are lifted is open and vulnerable to human pleas. Motivation clauses, seeking to persuade the Lord to help, are common in the Psalms. But the shape of the prayer as a whole in every part is itself a mode of appeal and persuasion, and thus it is indicative of the divine inclination to hear and respond.

• The endangerment of human existence is thus seen as something that arouses the zeal of God for its protection. The plight of the weak and the innocent, the sick and the oppressed, is the ground for God's intervention in the human scene (as in Ps. 35:10).

• The Psalms make claims about the relationship between God and Israel and its members. These involve expressions such as "my God," "the God of my salvation" (Ps. 25:5), "the sheep of your pasture" (74:1b), and so forth.

Core Testimony and Countertestimony

In his *Theology of the Old Testament*, Walter Brueggemann draws heavily on the legal metaphor of a courtroom and structures his analysis around the interplay of Israel's basic *core* testimony—a notion that reaches back, I think, to von Rad's fundamental formulation of the central claim and has generated a similar debate about the reality or historicity of what stands behind the witness—and a *counter*testimony that argues with and challenges the core testimony.[7] Neither core testimony nor countertestimony is confined to a particular part of the Old Testament. Both are found throughout. In this context, however, it is important to notice that the place where both forms of testimony are most strongly represented is in the Psalter. Indeed, precisely because of the way the Psalter incorporates both lament and praise or thanksgiving, and moves back and forth from one to the other in all sorts of ways, one may ask whether the questions and laments that are so common to the prayers for help are indeed a *counter*testimony at all. Perhaps they are rather such a reliance on the *fundamental claims* we find in the hymns of praise and elsewhere that one has to say that the lament psalms are in fact part of the *core* testimony.

As a specific example, one may take the frequent references to the steadfast love (*ḥesed*) of the Lord. Hermann Spieckermann has proposed that God's steadfast love may be perceived as the leitmotif of all of Scripture, and specifically the door into the theology of the Old Testament.[8] He makes a strong case for this claim. In his analysis he moves from (1) seeing the origin of Old Testament theology in the confessional formulation "The LORD, the LORD, a God merciful and gracious, slow to anger, and abounding in steadfast love . . . "—what Spieckermann calls the grace or mercy formula and what he regards as God's self-definition or *self-determination* toward *ḥesed*. Then (2) he turns to the Psalter as a depiction of *living in God's saving presence* because there "the good and merciful God proves to be the saving God."[9] Finally (3) in the prophets Spieckermann uncovers the steadfast love of the Lord still manifest in the face of Israel's betrayal and so now involving the dimension of *promise*. It is not surprising that the Psalter is the median point between the Pentateuch/Torah's announcement of God's self-determination and the Prophets' insistence that it shall not end. For, as Spieckermann notes, the *ḥesed* of the Lord is spoken about in the Psalter more extensively than in any other part of the Old Testament.[10]

In arguing that the nucleus of the confessional or grace formula of Exodus 34:6–7 proclaims Israel's God as a "God of love and faithfulness," Spieckermann remarks that *ḥesed* is "often explained by *ʾĕmet*. . . . The semantic spectrum coloured by *ḥesed* is marked by the terms grace, mercy, compassion, kindness, love, that of *ʾĕmet* by faithfulness and truth."[11] The combination of these terms—*ḥesed* and *ʾĕmet*—in speaking about the God of the Old Testament is extensive, but primarily in the Psalter. In a quite serious way, the depiction of the God who is self-defined as abounding in steadfast love and faithfulness is indeed thematic for the whole of Scripture, but one hears that theme in all its fullness especially in the Psalter. And even as the confessional formula makes its primary appearance in the Psalter, two other features impel one to see the primary testimony to the God of steadfast love there. One is the degree to which such steadfast love is a chief characteristic of Israel's God in both *lament* and *praise* psalms. The other is the way in which the dimension of promise and the future are significantly a part of the Psalms' celebration of the Lord's *ḥesed*. Let me then explicate the first of these two features, the *ḥesed* of

God in both lament and praise, and do so with reference to a particular and exemplary psalm.[12]

Psalm 86, a lament psalm or, as that genre is more accurately described, a prayer for help, contains one of the seven instances of the specific grace formula (v. 15) as well as one of the shorter variations on it (v. 5). This powerful prayer for help shows how a single psalm can articulate a comprehensive testimony to the character of God. Psalm 86 has often been ignored or summarily dismissed as of little significance because it draws so heavily on other texts and thus is not very original.[13] But as Hossfeld and Zenger have observed, the intertextuality of the psalm identifies it as "an artful *relecture* of existing texts."[14] Indeed, it is precisely because of its character as a *relecture* exemplifying in a paradigmatic way both the genres and the theology of the Psalter that I lift it up as one of the many psalms that articulate an understanding of the Lord of Israel and that resonate with voices all over the Old Testament.[15] Like many of the psalms, it draws on other texts and creates a conversation with many texts inside and outside the Psalter.

The first part of the Psalm is a series of calls to the Deity, cries for help, each of which is rooted in a particular reason, on the assumption that the reason set forth will move the Deity and impel God's saving and helping response:

> Incline your ear, O LORD, and answer me,
>> for I am poor and needy.
> Preserve my life, for I am devoted to you;
>> save your servant who trusts in you.
> You are my God; be gracious to me, O Lord,
>> for to you do I cry all day long.
> Gladden the soul of your servant,
>> for to you, O Lord, I lift up my soul.
> For you, O Lord, are good and forgiving,
>> abounding in steadfast love to all who call on you.
> Give ear, O LORD, to my prayer;
>> listen to my cry of supplication.
> In the day of my trouble I call on you,
>> for you will answer me. (86:1–7)

Three times in this first section, the psalmist speaks of calling out to God or crying out to God (*qārâ*), in each instance as a part of motivating and urging God to act:

For to you I call out [*qārâ*] all day long. (v. 3 AT)
For you, O Lord, are good and forgiving,
    full of steadfast love to all who call out [*qārâ*] to you. (v. 5 AT)
In the day of my trouble I call out [*qārâ*] to you,
    for you will answer me. (v. 7 AT)

While the sentences are the words of the sufferer uttered as grounds for appeal, the prayer at this point makes basic claims and assumptions about the Lord of Israel. This threefold outcry is in immediate conversation with the book of Deuteronomy at the point where we hear Moses compare Israel to the other nations and anticipate their envy because: "What other great nation has a god so near to it as the LORD our God is whenever we call [*qārâ*] to him?" (Deut. 4:7). The crying out is rooted in an assumption about the nearness of God, indeed something unique to the God of Israel and something to be envied by all the other nations, great or small. The human experience may actually be of God's distance and absence, as at the beginning of Psalm 22, but the theological assumption is of God's nearness to hear the outcry. Story after story in the Old Testament confirms that. As Norbert Lohfink has observed, the Deuteronomic statutes indicate that such calling to God is to be understood as the cry of the poor for God's help.[16] Confirmation of that understanding is provided by the first verse of Psalm 86, where the motivating appeal is "for I am poor and needy." In both contexts, Psalm 86 and Deuteronomy 4, the community hears of the nearness of God and the inclination of God's ear to hear and help the poor and needy.

The other motivating clauses in this part of the psalm are various affirmations of the *relationship* between this needy one and the Lord. The thematic claim of the Psalter, that God can be trusted to help, is asserted as the grounds for God's saving intervention in the situation of the needy, "the one trusting in you" (v. 2 AT). The central *covenantal* claim—"I will be your God, and you will be my people" (cf. Exod. 6:7; Jer. 30:22; etc.)—has its individual or personal manifestation in the claim of the psalmist in distress that "you are my God" (v. 2). The psalmist then affirms that in this relationship the Lord can be counted upon to respond to the cry for help—"for you will answer me" (v. 7)—even if experience is sometimes of silence and no answer to the cry (Ps. 22:1–2).

Appealing to God's Character

This does not exhaust the extent of the motivations in this part of Psalm 86. Yet its paradigmatic character is further indicated, as well as the function of these motivations, as a way of appealing to who and what God is. The appeal is to the character and nature of God, shown in verse 5 by one of the variations on the grace formula: "For you, O Lord, are good and forgiving, abounding in steadfast love to all who call on you" (v. 5). The sentence is quite pointed in claiming that the steadfast love of God is there for all who call on the Lord. The one whose way is constant and gracious, thus full of *ḥesed*, is one whose ears are attuned to the cry of the poor and the needy and whose way of acting in response is characteristically one of unfailing love, forgiveness, and goodness. The appearance of the term "good" (*ṭôb*) is an obvious connection into one of the other primary and most common formulas of the Old Testament and thus critical to its theology, that is, the paradigmatic prayer of thanksgiving: "O give thanks to the LORD, for he is good; for his steadfast love endures forever" (Ps. 106:1; etc.).[17] Psalm 86 joins these two pervasive theological formulas in its own particular way, including the dimension of forgiveness that is present also in the original divine self-determination formula of Exodus 34:6–7.

In the second section of Psalm 86, the psalmist moves now to praise and thanksgiving and in doing so moves also onto a larger plane, one that incorporates the gods and the nations, the heavens where the gods dwell, and even the underworld of Sheol:

> There is none like you among the gods, O Lord,
>> nor are there any works like yours.
> All the nations you have made shall come
>> and bow down before you, O Lord,
>> and shall glorify your name.
> For you are great and do wondrous things;
>> you alone are God.
> Teach me your way, O LORD,
>> that I may walk in your truth;
>> give me an undivided heart to revere your name.
> I give thanks to you, O Lord my God, with my whole heart,
>> and I will glorify your name forever.
> For great is your steadfast love toward me;
>> you have delivered my soul from the depths of Sheol. (86:8–13)

Here, as Hossfeld and Zenger have put it, "the psalm constructs a mighty stage on which it localizes the salvation implored by the petitioner, in order then to be able to describe its significance as the revealing of the unique God, YHWH [the Lord], and thus at the same time to depict the utterly inconceivable event—if *this* God were to turn his attention to a single human being, giving help and consolation. . . ."[18] The Lord of Israel is extolled for his wondrous works (v. 10), which are as much beyond compare as the Lord is beyond compare (v. 8), and include the making of the nations (v. 9).

At this point (86:8–12) several things thus happen: (1) The individual's story is placed on a cosmic plane. (2) The nations are in view as they are from the beginning of the Psalter (Ps. 2), thus identifying the universal dimension of the Lord's creative and redeeming works. (3) The three references to glorifying and revering "*your name*" (86:9, 11, 12), an act done by the psalmist *and* the nations, underscore the way in which the psalm, in its petitions and in its praise and thanksgiving, is set to unfold the character of God. (4) The plea "Teach me your way, O Lord, that I may walk in your truth" connects with both the beginning of the Psalter and the Torah as it embeds in the petition and praise a concern for faithful obedience to the divine instruction. (5) Such Torah obedience is underscored with the echoes of the First Commandment and the Shema as the psalmist declares, "You alone are God"; prays, "Unite my heart to fear your name" (AT); and offers thanks "with all my heart" (AT).

Finally the psalm concludes with a prayer for help once more, rooted in or motivated by a full articulation of the grace formula: "But you, O Lord, are a God merciful and gracious, slow to anger and abounding in steadfast love and faithfulness [*ḥesed weʾĕmet*]" (86:15). The one whose self-determined way is gracious is asked in this moment, when the psalmist is beset by the arrogant and the ruthless (*zēdîm, ʿârṣîm*), to turn and be gracious (*ḥānan*) to the one who now cries out for help. The psalmist concludes with a final prayer for a sign of God's "goodness" (*ṭôb*) against those who hate him and roots that in the memory and claim that "You, O Lord, have helped me and comforted me" (86:17 AT).

Between Memory and Hope

Psalm 86, like most of the psalms, lives between memory and hope, between the experience of God's way and the hope for it yet to come. Everything articulated is about "you, O Lord," and serves to glorify the name of the Lord even as it seeks to experience all that the name conveys;

if the Psalter is in some sense a *kleine Biblia*, a small Bible—as Luther famously labeled it—that is manifest in a variety of ways. The *Psalter as a whole* functions that way, particularly as a testimony to the character and way of the Lord of Israel. As we now know, from important work that has been done on the shape of the Psalter, its theological focus may be perceived in different ways, all of them large theological conceptions, and each of them a legitimate understanding of the book as a whole. One thinks, for example, of the ways that Gerald Wilson and James Mays have seen the whole of the Psalter or its center in an elaboration of the rule and kingship of God.[19] Or Erich Zenger's reading of the Psalter as *"itself the sanctuary* in which God shall be sought and praised and from which God's blessing and deliverance can go out."[20] Or Richard Kratz's impressive reading of the Psalter through the lens of its introduction and its structure as the torah of David, as in his words "So the Torah of YHWH and the Psalter are indeed not the same book but are in fact congruent, if not identical. According to Psalm 1, the Psalter makes explicit what the Pentateuch (and the Prophets) imply as the Torah of YHWH for the life of a righteous one."[21] It is not just the Psalter read as a whole book that offers a large vision of the glory of God and the human way. We have come, increasingly, to see how *pairs and groups* of Psalms serve as a full testimony to God's glory and resonate with the great themes and claims of Scripture as a whole. Examples are too numerous to go through. One has only to think of Psalms 103–104, which together are— to imitate Luther—*eine kleine systematische Theologie*, a small systematic theology, in poetic form. That becomes even more the case when one includes Psalms 102 and 105–107. Or Psalms 1–2 as they lead so fully into the themes of the Psalter.[22] Finally, *any particular psalm*, such as Psalm 86, can serve to glorify the name in its fullness, that is, to be a *kleine Biblia*. While the genres of the Psalter are varied, the psalms, as fully as the credos, are also the testimony, even the *core* testimony, to the nature and work of the God of Israel and the church. The Psalms create a conversation, both among themselves and with the rest of the Old Testament in its fullness.[23]

Having alluded to Luther's famous description of the Psalms as *eine kleine Biblia*,[24] I am reminded that one often finds versions of the New Testament with the Psalms printed at the back. This practice is often derided by biblical scholars as a dismissal of the rest of the Old Testament. That may indeed be implicit in such a publication. But equally implicit is a sense that in the Psalms one encounters the fullness of the revelation of the Old Testament.

If then, in all these ways, one may legitimately pair the Psalms with the New Testament to get at the whole of Scripture's revelation of the God, of Israel or describe them as a kind of "little Bible," then it is not finally sufficient to speak of the Psalms only as Israel's answer or response and thus as simply human words back to God. For they are fully *divine* word, revelatory of the fullness of God, formulaic and confessional, revealing of who God is and of God's way from creation to new creation. They are meant to be heard by the human community as much as they are meant to be heard by God. That is one of the special things about the Psalms in the Old Testament. They are both the human word to God and the word of God to human beings. In a large way, they are all we need to hear and all we need to say.

Chapter Six

Tender Mercies

One of the quietly memorable movies of the past quarter century is a simple story of two people. One is Mac Sledge, a once-famous country and Western singer who has hit the bottle and hit the skids, divorced from his wife, and in poor communication with his daughter, Sue Anne. The other person is the woman Mac meets, Rosa Lee, a young widow of a Vietnam soldier who is trying to support herself and raise her little boy, Sonny, by running a gas station / convenience store out in the flat, dry west Texas countryside. Mac is in the pits, and Rosa Lee does not have much going for her—except her faith. This is not a religious film. But even the blurb about the movie cannot avoid using theological language in trying to tell what it is about. It is a story of redemption, of the way in which Mac's encounter with Rosa Lee becomes a way out of the pit of drunkenness and despair.

What happens? How is Mac redeemed? Well, you know, there isn't much to tell. Not a lot happens. But a telling clue to what this movie is about appears in its title and the source of the title. Those who have seen the film will remember that its title, *Tender Mercies*, is taken from a moment when Mac is in a raging despair over his former wife's rejection of him and his effort to try to pick up his music again. In the face of that rage, Rosa Lee says to Mac: "Every night when I say my prayers, I thank the Lord for his blessings and his tender mercies to me. You and Sonny head the list."

There is a second *hidden* reference to the tender mercies of God in the movie, one of which perhaps only the screenwriter, Horton Foote, was aware. That night, after Rosa Lee has told Mac of her constant prayer, he disappears in anger, and she finally goes to bed, not knowing whether he will ever return. As she lies in bed, Rosa Lee recites two verses from Psalm 25:

> Shew me thy ways, O LORD;
>   teach me thy paths.
> Lead me in thy truth, and teach me:
>   for thou art the God of my salvation;
>   on thee do I wait all the day. (vv. 4–5 KJV)

Just as she starts to say the next line of the Psalm, Rosa Lee hears Mac coming in the door. So we do not get to hear her pray that next line: "Remember, O LORD, thy tender mercies and thy lovingkindnesses."

It is that daily prayer, and the conviction undergirding the prayer, that sustains Rosa Lee and molds her into a person whose own life is a quiet reflection of the tender mercies of God. Those tender mercies keep her, and through her they renew the life of Mac Sledge. Her unelaborated but real trust in the God whose tender mercies are new every day becomes the strong arm that pulls Mac from the downward slide of his life, that redeems his life from the pit.

I do not know what the director Bruce Beresford had in mind. But I do know what this movie is about. It is about the tender mercies of God, and it is not surprising that Rosa Lee's prayers are taken from the Psalms, where in her Bible (KJV) "tender mercies" repeatedly translates *raḥămîm* (cf. NRSV's "mercy" or "compassion"). The psalm that rings the changes on the tender mercies of God is the 103rd Psalm. In fact, it functions in many ways as the testimony of the soul that has cried out in Psalm 25, the psalm from which Rosa Lee finds her way (see below).

If Rosa Lee's Psalter-shaped piety takes me into Psalm 103, I also come to it in part to ask and try to answer the question Why this psalm? Why does this psalm hold us so? Why read this psalm at the beginning of the memorial service for Karl Barth after his death? What led Dietrich Bonhoeffer to select this text for the sermon at his wedding?[1] Why use this psalm on each of my family occasions, my sister's weddings, my parents' funerals? Why *this* psalm? I am not trying to solve a mystery, only to know what it is we hear and what it is that claims us as we sing the praise of God in the words of the One Hundred and Third Psalm.

The Structure and Movement of Psalm 103

We shall begin by looking at the psalm as a whole, its structure and movement, and conclude with a few theological reflections on what we have found.

Introduction: The Call to Praise (103:1–2)

The psalm begins and ends in thanksgiving and praise. In the Bible, the call to "bless the LORD" is a call to give thanks for what God has done. In Deuteronomy 8, Moses says to the people: "You shall eat your fill and bless the LORD your God for the good land that he has given you" (v. 10). Clearly that is what is going on here: "Forget not all his benefits" (KJV) parallels the second call to "Bless the LORD, O my soul." In the Psalms, thanks and praise blend together. Thus in Psalm 34 we read: "I will bless the LORD at all times; his praise shall continually be in my mouth." What we encounter here and generally in the psalms is a constant expression of gratitude that becomes adoration and praise, the exaltation of the God whose bounties or benefits, whose tender mercies, are set forth nowhere more abundantly than in this psalm.

The God of Tender Mercies (103:3–19)

Remembering the Lord's Bounties (103:3–5)

The opening verses, which set the intention of the psalm to evoke in as full a way as possible the praise of God, conclude with the exhortation: "And do not forget all his benefits [bounties]" (v. 2). In most songs of thanksgiving, one keeps from forgetting by telling the story of God's helping the psalmist to the larger community (e.g., Ps. 22:21b–31). In this case, one does so by telling the story to a "you," that "you" being the self who is addressed from the start. With that concluding address—"Do not forget all his benefits"—the psalm leads us into its subject: remembering and celebrating the God of tender mercies, the Lord of great bounties. Thanksgiving here and always is an act of remembering.

The dialogue with the soul continues by listing "all his bounties," employing a typical hymnic form with a series of participles characterizing the Lord who is praised as one who forgives, who heals, who redeems, and so on. Notice how God's attributes are presented: not in absolute terms, as in a general theological statement, but with a relative and personal "you." The "you" that is the human self is being reminded of all that God has done for "you"—your iniquity, your diseases, your life, your youth. One may extrapolate individual reference from that, but only as a secondary move. To begin with, as in the case of Rosa Lee, it is an intimate conversation with the self about all the mercies this one has known from the Lord.

Those mercies are recounted in verses 3–5, in a series of paired clauses, the parallelism suggesting that the A and B parts of the lines are to be seen in relation to each other. It is not just an extended list of divine attributes, like the catechism: "God is a spirit, infinite, eternal, and unchangeable in his being, wisdom, power, holiness, justice, goodness, and truth."[2] The memory of God's bounties is caught in the paired expressions. Thus the soul is reminded of the following acts of divine mercy: forgiveness and healing (v. 3), redemption and steadfast love (v. 4), provision and renewal (v. 5).

The Ways and Deeds of the Lord (103:6–18)

Verse 6 is clearly transitional, and this in two ways. First, with "all who are oppressed," the psalm turns from the self to the wider human community. Second, it looks both backward and forward. Looking backward, it concludes the participial list of God's bounties: "The LORD is the one who does righteous deeds, and acts of justice for all the oppressed" (AT). This theme, which defines the Lord of the Psalms, is never more explicitly or simply said than in this verse. In addition, this fundamental claim about the Lord also looks forward as God's righteous deeds and acts of justice, the Lord's bountiful ways, are now remembered in the context of Israel's life before the Lord:

> He made known his ways to Moses,
>   his acts to the people of Israel. (v. 7)

The connection or transition between the earlier verses and the rest of the Psalm is further reflected in the allusion to the "oppressed" or "wronged" for whom the Lord has wrought justice (v. 6). That is the community to whom the psalmist belongs by definition, as much as to the sinful and the sick, the ones in the Pit and those who are satisfied with good (cf. vv. 3–4). But the oppressed are now also a particular community, the people of Israel, who through Moses and through their own experience came to know the ways and deeds of the Lord. "He made known his ways to Moses" is a quite specific reference back to Exodus 33:13, where Moses intercedes for the people who have broken covenant and the First Commandment in their fashioning of the golden calf: "Now if I have found favor in your sight, *show me your ways*, so that I may know you and find favor in your sight." What follows then is the Lord's passing before Moses and proclaiming:

> "The LORD, the LORD,
> a God merciful and gracious,
> slow to anger,
> and abounding in steadfast love and faithfulness,
> keeping steadfast love for the thousandth generation,
> forgiving iniquity and transgression and sin,
> yet by no means clearing the guilty,
> but visiting the iniquity of the parents
> upon the children and the children's children,
> to the third and the fourth generation." (Exod. 34:6–7)

These verses became Israel's clearest and most ancient confession, and they may be regarded as the foundational theological statement of Scripture, out of which everything else flows. So we may see verses 8 to 13 of Psalm 103 as a rearticulation, an elaboration of this ancient confession. It is as close as one can come to an ancient creed or to the Old Testament answer to the catechism question: "What is God?"

The ways and deeds of the Lord, already identified in the dialogue with the soul, are now laid out in verse 8 in terms of the ancient confession: "The LORD is merciful and gracious, slow to anger and abounding in steadfast love." What follows in the next ten verses is an elaboration of this claim, about God's slowness to anger (vv. 9–10), how abundant God's steadfast love is (vv. 11 and 17), and in verse 13 the character of God's gracious and merciful compassion. All of this is an effort to say how the grace, mercy, and love of God are experienced by the soul or self (vv. 1–5), by the oppressed (v. 6), by Israel (v. 7), and now, as the next verses will express it, by "us." With these first-person-plural pronouns, the contemporary reader/congregation is drawn into the psalm. Note the movement: What begins as a conversation between the psalmist and his soul, and then becomes a characterization of the God of Israel, now is seen to have to do with *us*, and with us in the two dimensions of our existence that are most problematic: our *sin* (vv. 9–13) and our *transience* (vv. 14–18). The psalmist's theological voice is first negative in its claims about what God does not do (vv. 9–10), then metaphorical in its comparisons (vv. 11–16), and finally climaxing in the positive claim in verses 17–18 for what God does: the extravagance beyond measure of God's love.

The claim "He will not always accuse [contend], nor will he keep his anger forever" (v. 9) responds to a question that is implicit in the whole history of Israel: Is God's judgment God's last word to a wayward people? The question is set forth in Jeremiah 3 when Israel calls out to the Lord: "'My Father, you are the friend of my youth—will he be angry forever, will he be indignant to the end?'" (vv. 4–5). To this question both Isaiah and Jeremiah give the answer: "For not forever will I judge/contend; and not forever will I be angry" (Isa. 57:16 AT); and "Return, faithless Israel, says the LORD. I will not look on you in anger, for I am merciful, says the LORD; I will not be angry forever" (Jer. 3:12). This answer is the starting point for the elaboration of the *ḥesed* of the Lord in Psalm 103:3.

But if the question "Will the LORD be angry forever?" evokes the claim of the psalmist: "He will not always contend/accuse, nor will he keep his anger forever," this leaves the question for any reader: "*Well, then, how long will the LORD keep the LORD's anger?*" The prophets and the psalmists answer this question. It is the same answer each time: "*Just for a moment.*" And in each instance, as in Psalm 103, that moment of anger is placed in stark contrast to the extent of God's love and favor. So Isaiah proclaims the divine assurance (Isa. 54:7–8):

> For a brief moment [*regaʿ*] I abandoned you,
>   but with great compassion I will gather you.
> In overflowing wrath for a moment [*regaʿ*]
>   I hid my face from you,
> but with everlasting love [*ḥesed ʿōlām*, just as in Ps. 103:17]
>   I will have compassion on you.
>   [like a father's compassion for his children in Ps. 103:13]

The psalmist in Psalm 30, calling the people to praise the Lord, makes exactly the same point (v. 5):

> For his anger is but for a moment [*regaʿ*];
>   his favor is for a lifetime.
> Weeping may linger for the night,
>   but joy comes with the morning.

The judgment of a just God is a reality; the anger of God at a people who fail to live by the covenant is to be expected. What matters is that even so, it is only for a moment. The psalmist in Psalm 103 underscores this stark difference by pointing out that divine recompense is not what one would normally expect. God's recompense is not "payment in kind," or "tit for tat." It is not in accordance with the extent and character of our iniquities. The repayment for our sins takes the form of the bounties or benefits of which the psalmist has spoken earlier. Divine justice is overwhelmed by or takes the form of divine grace. Why does God deal with us in this way? Two reasons are given—see the "for" at the beginnings of verses 11 and 14. The first reason has to do with the way God is, and the second with the way we are. Let us look at them.

In verse 11 the psalmist joins two images. One, "For your steadfast love [*ḥesed*] is higher than the heavens"—is a picture of God's *ḥesed* as being on a scale comparable only to that of the heavens above the earth. A second image is one of comparative power, as in battle: "So his steadfast love has prevailed [or is powerful] over those who fear him." This tender mercy, this loving-kindness, God's steadfast love, which is as vast as the universe, is more powerful than our sins and in this sense has won the battle over those who fear God. The vastness of God's grace and the overwhelming power of God to deal mercifully with our sins is then articulated with another comparison in verse 12. How has this *ḥesed* prevailed over our iniquities? The answer is emphatic: The Lord has gotten rid of our sins by tossing them as far as the east is from the west, as far away as is possible for the mind to conceive.

As if the claim has not been made strongly enough, we hear in verse 17 that "the *ḥesed* of the LORD is from everlasting to everlasting to those who fear him" (AT). In addition to the spatial imagery, the psalmist now uses temporal categories to express the vastness of the grace and mercy of God: as high as the heavens above the earth, as far as the east from the west, and now from everlasting to everlasting.

Then in the parallel colon of verse 17, the psalmist says "and his righteousness to children's children." That last expression in connection with the grace and righteousness of God echoes once again the confessional formulary of Exodus 34, but with a radical reversal. To this point the psalm has expounded the meaning of the first part of the formulary: "a God merciful and gracious, slow to anger, and abounding in steadfast love and faithfulness," and then we have what follows that: "keeping steadfast love for the thousandth generation, forgiving iniquity and transgression and sin, yet by no means clearing the guilty, but visiting the iniquity of the parents upon the children and the children's children to the third and fourth generation" (Exod. 34:6–7). Not so in the psalm. The *ḥesed* is from everlasting to everlasting, God's righteousness to children's children. The psalm modifies the ancient confession and extends the steadfast love of the Lord. It has no end. One cannot help but think of Romans 8:39: "Neither height, nor depth, nor anything else in all creation, will be able to separate us from the love of God in Christ Jesus our Lord."

Still the psalmist has not finished the effort to convey something of the vastness of the grace and mercy of God. A further comparison is made in verse 13, this time not in terms of time or space but out of a familiar human relationship, the father and his children. If the previous comparisons serve to catch us by their extravagant imaging of the scope and immeasurability of God's grace, the third is designed to catch us by our experience as parent and child. From both directions we know something of the tenderness and compassion of that relationship, as children, being loved and forgiven for our mistakes; as parents, loving and caring for our children despite their frailties and errors.

Then in verses 14–16 we are given the second reason why the Lord does not deal with us according to our sins but as a compassionate parent. It is God's awareness, God's constant remembrance that we are *mortal creatures*, whose days are like grass that fades and disappears before the wind (cf. Isa. 40:6–8; Ps. 90). Not to be missed in verse 14 is the allusion to Genesis 2:7. "He knows how we were made [formed]; he remembers that we are dust." It is our created nature that God takes account of—our humanity, our finitude, our mortality. The Lord "knows" who and what we are, and God's gracious, extravagant treatment of us is in light of that. Earlier, the explanation for God's compassionate treatment has focused on dealing with our human sin. Now we hear that the love of God is in behalf of our mortality and because we are mere dust. The human creature, "we," may disappear like a flower before the wind. "But the steadfast love of the LORD is from everlasting to everlasting" (v. 17). We might risk saying that divine grace overwhelms our mortality as well as our sin, and that in Psalm 103 we have an anticipation of the gospel: the victory of God's grace not only over sin but also over death.

The Lord's Rule over All (103:19)

If the Psalm finds its center in verse 8 with the quotation of the confessional formulary, and its elaboration in verses 8–18, it reaches its peak in verse 19 with the announcement "The LORD has established his throne in the heavens, and his kingdom rules over all." The sudden shift of theme places all that has been said to this point in the context of the larger Psalter, and particularly Book IV, of which this psalm is a central part. Let me elaborate that with reference to the verses that follow and conclude the psalm.

Conclusion: The Expanded Call to Praise (103:20–22)

The call to praise that is heard at the beginning of the psalm—"Bless the LORD"—is heard again but now with a scope not imagined at the beginning of the psalm. Now the call addresses all the hosts of heaven, all the works of creation, everything and everywhere under the Lord's reign. What began in an address to the soul/self and a recollection of how the soul has experienced the *ḥesed* of the Lord has moved out now to an overwhelming claim about the Lord's rule "over all." The psalm, beginning in a dialogue with the self and then expanding in verses 10–18 to speak of "us," now lets "us" know that all of this is about the kingdom of God, the nature and character of the rule of God.

Then, at the very end, the psalm returns to its beginning, with "Bless the LORD, O my soul," which provides a bridge to the next psalm, a psalm in celebration of creation, which also begins and ends "Bless the LORD, O my soul." It is as if the psalmist says: "All right, let's do that again, only now it is God as creator and all God's marvelous works of creation that elicit the praise and thanksgiving of the soul."

Theological Reflections on Psalm 103

The Realism of Psalm 103

One reason this psalm catches and holds our attention is to be found in its *realism* about the human condition, and this in several ways:

1. It is straightforward about our *finitude and mortality*. We are here for a while, flourishing, enjoying life, and then we are gone.

2. The psalm is equally realistic about the condition of human life before it fades and disappears. We are beset by *two powers that destroy us*. The first is our mortality, and the other is the power of sin, though the psalm speaks no more of sin as a power than it does of death. In neither case are these realities externalized. They have to do with us. So the psalm speaks personally about the reality of sin, not abstractly but about "*our* sins," "*our* iniquities," and "*our* transgressions."

3. The psalm is realistic also in its awareness that we are done in not only by our mortality and by our sins but also by *sickness and disease*, by *suffering and oppression*, forces outside ourselves that attack us and undo us.

The parallel conjoining of "forgives all your iniquity" with "heals all your diseases" is a crucial theological move. For here we see both sin-guilt and sickness-suffering held together as the fundamental human condition. The human problem to which God responds is not either sin-guilt or sickness-suffering: it is both. One sees these combined and intermixed all through the Psalms, as in 25:18: "See my affliction and my trouble, and forgive all my sin" (AT), and 41:4: "As for me, I said, 'O LORD, be gracious to me; heal me, for I have sinned against you." Similarly, suffering and guilt, healing and forgiveness come together in the story of Jesus and the paralytic (Mark 2:1–12). They are completely intertwined as Jesus both forgives and heals. Thus our understanding of God's dealing with our condition is not finally reduced to one or the other. As I was writing these words, the daily newspaper told of a father's misery or suffering over his son's suicide but also his sense of guilt because he did not call him before going to work that day as he usually did.

4. The realism of the psalm is manifest also as the psalmist's exultation in the one "who redeems your life from the Pit [and] crowns you with steadfast love and mercy" (v. 4) joins the deliverance from death with the *divine blessing of life*. In Psalm 8 the question "What are human beings?" is answered with "You crowned them with glory and honor." But suffering Job also asked, 'What are human beings, that you make so much of them?" and answered, "He has stripped my glory from me, and taken the crown from my head" (Job 7:17; 19:9). So also the people in Lamentations 5:16 utter a lament: "The crown has fallen from our head; woe to us, for we have sinned." It is this experience, when human existence has lost its glory and honor, to which the psalmist alludes in celebrating God's restorative actions.

5. Nor is human life possible without the flourishing that comes as *God's providence sustains and renews* us day by day: "Who satisfies you with good as long as you live so that your life is renewed like the eagle's" (v. 5)

Anthropology Leading to Theology

All that I have just said about the Psalm's realistic and rich depiction of human existence shows that, in Psalm 103, the avenue to theology is via anthropology. Apparently all that is said about the human is in order to speak about the character and reality of God. To take one example, consider verse 14: "For he knows how we were made [our frame]; he remembers that we are dust." The one formed out of the dust does not escape the mortality that is an outcome of the garden story in Genesis.

Now, however, set over against that outcome is the transcendent and overwhelming love of God. So if the psalm is realistic and truthful about our mortality, our sin, our pain, our life and death, then we have reason to be confident it is also realistic and truthful about the God whose praises are sung in these verses. Our cries of pain and guilt are penultimate. The last words in truth, the last words now, the last words then, the last words always, are the songs of joy and praise to the God whose mercies are new every morning and fresh every day.

God's Bounties: Limited or Unlimited?

We must not skip over what I would call the theological problem of the psalm: the conflict between the limitless and the limited. The *limitless* is reflected in *two ways*, one being the use of "all" at critical points: "who forgives *all* your iniquity, who heals *all* your diseases" (v. 3); who "works vindication and justice for *all* who are oppressed" (v. 6). The other way is the extravagant and unlimited manifestation of the grace of God, the steadfast love of the Lord from everlasting to everlasting (esp. vv. 8, 11–12, 17). Over against this limitless experience of that love is the critical *qualification* that we hear three times, as much as in any psalm: "toward those who fear him" (vv. 11, 13, 17). "The steadfast love of the LORD is from everlasting to everlasting on those who fear him" (v. 17). This final usage is expanded and elaborated: "to those who keep his covenant and remember to do his commandments" (v. 18).

In juxtaposing these two aspects of God's bounties as "limited" and "limitless," Psalm 103 brings together two fundamental paradigms of the biblical representation of God.[3] One is the Abrahamic paradigm—patriarchal, personal-familial—that we find in Genesis: God as giver of conception, birth, nurture, guidance and protection, and the divine source and sanction for the kindly virtues of *ḥesed* and *raḥămîm* (steadfast love and mercy). The other is the Mosaic covenantal paradigm, political and contractual, not familial in nature, where the failure of the covenantal relationship evokes divine jealousy and anger. The Sinai covenant comes into view at verse 7 with its reference to Moses, and becomes even more explicit with the several references to "those who fear him," especially as elaborated in verse 18: "to those who keep his covenant and remember to do his commandments." The story of Moses and Israel has its structure in the covenant, with its sanctions. Psalm 103 recognizes that those life-or-death sanctions "have become tempered by the compassionate ethos of the ancestral paradigm."[4] The point is accentuated in the psalm by the not-at-all accidental comparison of the Lord's way to that of a parent with a child: "as a father has compassion for his children" (Ps. 103:13). There is no limit to the grace of God, the compassion and tender mercies as high as the heavens, as far as east from west, and forgiving *all* your iniquities, healing *all* your diseases. That unfathomable and eternal love is manifest and experienced by a community that is not defined ethnically or any other way except by their fear of the Lord, that is, by those who live in awe and trust of this God, who follow the Lord's ways in the world. Here and in two or three other places, all in the Psalms, we hear so clearly the union of God's steadfast love and our fear of the Lord as the central reality of our existence: "Let those who fear the LORD say, 'His steadfast love endures forever'" (118:4); "Truly the eye of the LORD is on those who fear him, on those who hope in his steadfast love" (33:18). To hope in that extravagant love is precisely what it means to fear the Lord: that love and grace, that compassion and mercy can be counted upon. Here as much as anywhere in Scripture, the oneness of gospel and law, of love and obedience, are evident. And the parental image is crucial to our theology, to our understanding of God's way with us, even as the image of child is crucial to our anthropology, to our understanding of how we are the Lord's.

The Psalms Context for Psalm 103

The most important development in Psalms study over the past twenty years is the extended focus on the Psalter as the context for each individual Psalm. We no longer read them simply each on its own, because it is often evident that individual psalms are in conversation with one another, often by their place in the book but also by their language and concerns. That is certainly the case with Psalm 103. In an important essay, Walter Brueggemann helps us see the movement in the Psalter from the lament of Psalm 25 and its questions about the steadfast love of the Lord to the large claims of the enduring love of the Lord in Psalm 103.[5] Brueggemann is surely correct, for these psalms echo each other again and again.

While Psalm 103 has many resonances with other psalms, it is most noticeably and significantly connected to the psalms that immediately precede and follow it. Psalm 102 presents itself as a kind of paradigmatic lament or cry for help, with its unique superscription not referring to any historical figure or cultic moment but identifying the psalm simply as "A prayer of one afflicted, when faint and pleading before the LORD." Thus while Psalm 103 can respond to any of the prayers of the Psalter, it is so connected to Psalm 102 that one may see 102 as opening issues and questions to which 103 offers the answer or solution. Psalm 102 cries out of a situation of distress and illness: "For my days pass away like smoke, and my bones burn like a furnace" (102:3), all of this "because of your indignation and anger" (v. 10). Psalm 103 makes it clear that divine anger, experienced by the pleading psalmist in Psalm 102, is not the final word, not even the large word. The Lord will not be angry forever. The awareness of mortality and sin is large in Psalm 102, there experienced as the particular fate of the lamenting psalmist: "My days pass away like smoke" (v. 3). Over against that, Psalm 103 speaks of the forever and enduring steadfast love of the Lord to those who, like the psalmist of Psalm 102, fear the Lord.

But however close may be the connections between Psalms 102 and 103, the pairing of Psalms 103 and 104 is so clear and intentional that it cannot be overlooked in the interpretation of either psalm. The exhortation: "Bless the LORD, O my soul" occurs only four times in the Bible: at the beginning and ending of Psalms 103 and 104, a redactional device telling us to hold these psalms together and read them together. The God whose redeeming grace is so completely elaborated in Psalm 103 is the same Lord who created the heavens and the earth, the seas and the mountains, the birds and the badgers, who put the waters in their place and made habitats for the animals, who satisfies all creatures with good even as is done for the life of each of us (Ps. 103:5). The last exhortation to praise of Psalm 103 before the final "Bless the LORD, O my soul" is a call to "bless the LORD, all his works in all places of his dominion." What are all those works and all those places? Keep reading. You won't really know until you have read Psalm 104.

Praise as the Vehicle of Theology

Psalm 103 thus attests that the primary vehicle of theology is praise and doxology. It is in giving glory to God that we both learn and announce what we know about the God who made us and has loved us. In the hymns and songs of thanksgiving of the Psalter and elsewhere, the call to praise and thanksgiving is always given a reason and basis for praise: an extended description of what God has done, how God has been present, what God is like. In so doing, the people of God learn who God is and declare it to a larger audience. Every hymn is a theological lesson, an effort to characterize and understand the Lord in order to give glory to and enjoy the Lord. At one and the same time, the community in its praise both gives glory to God and says what it believes and knows about the Lord of Israel and the church.

And what Psalm 103 portrays as the height of God's way with us—"The steadfast love of the LORD is from everlasting to everlasting"—becomes the heart of the short form of Israel's praise and ours: "O give thanks to the LORD for he is good; his steadfast love endures forever." No single verse of Scripture is repeated more often in the Bible (e.g., 2 Chr. 5:13; 7:3, 6; Ezra 3:10–11; Jer. 33:11; Pss. 106:1; 107:1; 118:1; etc.). If you do not have any other verse to carry with you, if you need a way to hold and remember and say all that matters in as simple a form as possible, there you have it: "O give thanks to the LORD, for the LORD is good; God's steadfast love endures forever" (AT). There is where our theology begins and ends.

Chapter Seven

The First Catechism Question and the Theology of the Psalter

There are few pieces of Reformed doctrine more familiar than the first question of the Westminster Shorter Catechism. It asks very simply: "What is the chief end of man?" And it answers just as briefly: "Man's chief end is to glorify God, and to enjoy him forever." I expect the brevity of the question and the answer has much to do with its familiarity. At least it is one of only two questions from the Catechism that I can remember from my youth when I memorized the whole thing. (The other one was "What is sin?") I don't think, however, that is all there is to the matter. I expect even more valuable than its brevity is the way in which this short question-answer has encapsulated so clearly what may be said to be the heart of the matter. It is not accidental that it is the first question. In some ways it is the first and last question, the bottom line. Why are we here? Well, there it is, as simply and eloquently as one can put it.

In this chapter I explore the richness and meaning of this Catechism question from the perspective of the Psalter, and I do mean the Psalter. While the history of Psalms study has focused primarily on the individual psalms and their types or genres, much of the more recent study has concerned itself with *the book as a whole*, both its literary formation and its message as a book. Following that direction, I want to suggest some ways in which the theology of the Psalter as a whole serves as an elaboration of or a commentary on the Catechism answer about our chief end, our goal and purpose, as human beings.

The richness of the Psalter inevitably means there is not simply one way of reading it as a whole. Various perspectives on the movement and shape of the Psalter have been identified, each one generally uncovering

85

features in the book that serve to set forth and develop the particular perspective. I am going to take up two of these perspectives that help us see what the Psalter is about and in so doing serve to flesh out the answer to the Catechism question about our chief end. One of these perspectives is particularly attentive to the *movement* of the Psalter and *how it ends*. The other looks particularly at *how it begins* and what signals are given there and developed in the rest of the Psalter to answer the question What's it all about? As with many books, one learns much about what is going on in this one by attending to how it begins and how it ends.

Opening the Way: Psalms 1–2 Introduce the Psalter

So we shall start at the beginning. The character and function of Psalms 1 and 2 as introduction to the Psalter is widely recognized. All the rest of the Psalms in Book I of the Psalter (i.e., Pss. 3–41), have some kind of superscription unless the two psalms are meant to be read together, as in the case of Psalms 9 and 10 and Psalms 32 and 33. But there is no superscription about David or musical note for either Psalm 1 or Psalm 2. The two psalms themselves are the superscription for the Psalter. They are linked by various similar words or expressions and especially by the way Psalm 1 begins "Blessed is the one who does not walk in the council of the wicked" (AT) and the way Psalm 2 ends with a similarly formed conclusion: "Blessed is the one who takes refuge in him" (AT). In so doing each psalm identifies a central theme of the Psalter: the problem of the wicked and their oppressive ways, and the possibility of finding refuge and protection in the Lord.

Let me begin with Psalm 2 and the agenda it sets for the Psalter before I turn to Psalm 1. Psalm 2 is a royal psalm, probably in connection with the coronation of a king. Two things are crucial outcomes from the way this psalm sets up what lies ahead in the Psalter. One is the indication that whatever else is going on in the Psalms that follow, serious attention will be focused on the world of politics and government, the interaction of kings and nations. The psalms are not simply individual prayers for personal use and having to do only with personal situations. They deal with the whole of our life, in community as well as in private. And while the psalm is focused on the appointment of the king as God's son and ruler of the nations, from beginning to end it is clear that the matter at hand is the rule of the Lord. That is evident, for example, in verse 6, where the Lord announces to the nations and the kings of the earth: "I have set my king on Zion, my holy mountain" (AT).

Several things are to be observed. The *divine activity through the king as God's chosen* is underscored by the initial "I have set" and the pronominal form "my king." A further dimension is added at this point, one that is crucial to the function of the psalm as introduction to what follows. That is the *divine choice of Zion*, here seen in its dual character, which will be evident throughout the rest of the Psalter: it is (1) the place of the Lord's dwelling, "my holy mountain," and also (2) the place where the Lord's anointed rules in behalf of the Lord. Throughout the Psalter, the reader will encounter Jerusalem as political center of the Lord's rule but also as the place where the Lord dwells, where the house of the Lord is to be found, and where one may come into God's presence (e.g., Pss. 15; 23; 24; 73:17; etc.). It is the holy place of the Lord's presence and the Lord's rule.

Verse 10, as it begins with "Now therefore, O kings, be wise," marks a conclusion or implication to be drawn from all that has been said: The kings of the earth are to smarten up and act wisely. The content of such wise action is clear and specific and to the point: "Serve the LORD with fear." That is what the whole Bible is about, of course, and it is not a surprise to hear it as a primary directive at the beginning of the Psalter. Such basic but complete instruction is reflective of the introductory words in Psalm 1 and is here understood to be not simply the way of Israel but also the way of all nations. The goal of the Psalter is encompassed in the words "Serve the LORD with fear." Already the Psalms are letting us know what is the human purpose, encompassing nations and kingdoms as well as individuals. It is to live in reverence before the Lord.

The chords we hear in Psalm 2 ring throughout the Psalter. I will refer, however, to only one other important reverberation in the rest of the Psalter. Book II of the Psalter ends the prayers of David with a royal psalm declaring the nature of God's rule as carried out by the king (Ps. 72). In it the nations pay homage and service because this king delivers the poor and the weak from oppression and violence and gives them help, a central dimension not only of God's way but also of God's very being, as evident from Psalm 82. In a sense the psalm is the high point of the royal theology of the Psalter.

Things are different, however, several Psalms onward, at the end of Book III of the Psalter. The last psalm in Book III, Psalm 89, concludes as a lament, with the community complaining that God has rejected and spurned the king and has renounced the covenant with David (vv. 38–45). It ends with the actual complaint of the king in two parts: a question: "Lord, where is your steadfast love of old?" (v. 49); and a petition: "Remember, O Lord, how your servant is taunted; how I bear in my bosom the insults of the peoples, with which your enemies taunt, O LORD, with which they taunted the footsteps of your anointed" (vv. 50–51). The question is sounded especially acutely because of the claims that have been made in the first part of the psalm. No psalm declares God's steadfast love more repeatedly than this one, three times as characteristic of the Lord forever (vv. 1, 2, 14), and three more times as the Lord's promise to keep steadfast love with David and his descendants forever—even if they sin (vv. 24, 28, 33). Verse 49 now asks, in effect, "What about that?" As the petition makes clear, kingship has gone under. The note of lament and complaint to God with which Book III ends is accentuated by the immediately preceding Psalm 88, the bleakest of all the laments, with its own question: "Is your steadfast love declared in the grave?" (v. 11). The human voice and the royal voice are at their nadir: their only word is complaint to and against God. At this point in the Psalter, we have reached a crisis.

Book IV (Pss. 90–106) seeks to address that crisis. While it starts in Psalm 90 with an acknowledgment of the transience and sinfulness of human life, Book IV—and in some sense the Psalter as a whole—reaches its climax in the series of Psalms 93–99, a group of hymns of praise whose one intention is to assert and describe what is meant by their key and repeated phrase: "The LORD reigns" (AT).[1] The assumption that everything is down the drain with the fall of the Davidic house and the overthrow of the human ruler is countered in an extensive and massive way here. The Psalter reaches its climax in this declaration that it is really the Lord who rules over all, a rule that is eternal and over against all human failures, transience, and sinfulness. Over and over these psalms declare that God is a great God and a great king above all gods and human rulers. The psalms declare the coming rule of God and judgment over all the nations, a rule that is carried out in righteousness and thus is the hope of the righteous even when human kingship fails.

We must not forget, however, that Psalm 2 with its reverberations is only part of the introduction to the Psalter, indeed the second part. So we need to turn back to the first introductory note, which is Psalm 1. Together with Psalm 2, the First Psalm sets the agenda of the Psalter, letting us know what to look for and what it is about.

The Righteous and the Wicked

One of its entrées into the Psalter as a whole is the First Psalm's identification of the way of the wicked and the way of the righteous, as well as their respective fates. Sometimes they are given other names, such as evildoers or fools, and God-fearers or the wise, but how these two groups or categories of people act, the way they go, is very much the subject of the Psalter. Further, for Psalm 1, the "way" has to do with both the path of life one chooses and one's ultimate fate, that is, one's end. Both of these dimensions of the way are the subject matter of the Psalms, beginning in Book I (e.g., Pss. 5:4–6, 12; 9:15–18; 10:2–11; 11:2–3, 5, 6–7). The focus on these two groups is evident also in the great number of laments in Book I and the first half of the Psalter, for it is especially in these psalms that both the wicked and the righteous come to the fore. Throughout the Psalter, the righteous are often to be equated with or found among the poor, the weak, and the needy (e.g., Pss. 14:5–6; 86:1; 109:22) as well as imitators of God's way (e.g., Pss. 12:5; 14:6; 34:6; 113:7; 132:15; 140:12) as they support the poor and the weak (e.g., Pss. 41:1; 112:9). Psalm 41, which concludes Book I, forms a bracket around the first book with its opening sentence "Happy/Blessed are those who consider the poor" echoing the beginning of the Psalter "Happy/Blessed are those who do not follow the way of the wicked." Thus the beginning of Book I and the Psalter identify the way not to go, and the end of Book I shows the right way to go. The reverberations of this opening to the Psalter do not end there. Especially noticeable is how the final coda of praise (Pss. 146–150) lifts up once more the contrast between the two ways and their outcomes, as in Psalm 146: "The LORD loves the righteous, . . . but the way of the wicked he brings to ruin" (vv. 8–9).

The Law of the Lord at the Center

As a pointer of the way for the reader, Psalm 1 sets the Psalter before us as a *book of instruction*, with the law of the Lord as the focus of attention. That direction is accentuated in several ways in what follows:

1. Within Psalm 1 itself, "the law of the LORD" is emphasized by the repetition of that expression in verse 2 and by the "day and night" meditation on the law by the one who delights in it. With such an introduction, one cannot avoid seeing what follows as instructive in that regard.

2. The Psalter is organized into five books, suggesting a comparison with the five books of the Torah. As such, the Torah is constantly in the mind of the reader of the Psalter, but the Psalter itself is seen to be Torah-like in its shape and thus capable of providing similar instruction about the way of righteousness.

3. Looming large over the whole Psalter is Psalm 119, which for 176 verses exalts the law and its positive benefits. It has been suggested that

at one point the Psalter may have begun with Psalm 1 and ended with Psalm 119. Whether or not that is the case, Psalm 119 functions as a landmark or beacon, dominating the whole Psalter. It forms an inclusion with Psalm 1 not only in its primary subject matter of the law of the Lord, but also as it begins with two "Blessed/Happy" sentences, the first one of which echoes the beginning of Psalm 1: "Blessed are those blameless in the way, the ones walking in the law of the LORD" (AT). Nearly every line includes some term for the law, and repeatedly the psalm speaks of the way or path. Because Psalm 119 is also permeated by a lament, not always recognized by readers, it serves to make clear that the prayer for help is part of the instruction of the Psalter. The Psalter is at one and the same time a prayer book and a book of meditation and instruction.

Delight in Keeping the Lord's Instruction

Critical to Psalm 1's role as a directive for the reader of the Psalter is the *positive* view of the law of the Lord. The psalm does not call for *obedience* to the law—though that is assumed—but for *delight* in it. The positive effects of the law are laid out in the image of the tree transplanted by the water, which is marked by its sudden fruitfulness, its stability and durability. This is in contrast to the ephemeral, vapid nothingness of the way of the wicked, as useless, impermanent, and meaningless as chaff! This positive view of the law and its benefits is present wherever the law is talked about in the Psalter. Not only does Psalm 119 make this point again and again, but it is also at the heart of Psalm 19, which recounts in detail the beneficial characteristics of "the law of the LORD," its precepts and decrees, comparing them to the finest gold and the sweetest honey (19:10; a dual comparison that recurs in Ps. 119:72, 103). To put it in the succinct words of the Psalm: "In keeping them there is great reward" (19:11). In similar fashion, Psalm 1 describes those who greatly "delight" in the Lord's commandments as blessed or happy, indeed to be envied. The way of the torah, the way of the Lord, is the way of happiness.

Listening to the End: Movement from Prayer to Praise

If in the Psalter, as in most books, the beginning is an important clue to what lies ahead and what is going on in the book, the same is certainly true of the ending of the book of Psalms. But the ending always grows out of what has gone before and cannot be fully comprehended apart from knowing what has led to the conclusion. So we now want to look at the Psalter as a whole in terms of another movement, one that provides another lens for viewing the theology of the book and its elaboration of the answer to the Catechism question about our chief end as human beings.

The genre of lament is the single largest type of psalm in the Psalter. Some 70 odd psalms are generally assigned to this genre. Here is the prayer form of the Psalms, what is surely meant when the psalms and other texts speak of *tĕpillâ,* "prayer." It is also what is in view in many other expressions found in the psalms, such as references to "crying out" or "calling." Again and again the psalmist cries out to the Lord and calls for the Lord to answer (Pss. 4:1; 13:3; 27:7; 86:1; 102:2; etc.). Even more often we hear the psalmist speaking of God as answering or not answering a personal prayer (3:4; 17:6; 18:41; etc.). In a number of places, the claim that God answers prayer is definitive, for example: "You who answer prayer!" (65:2). "The eyes of the LORD are on the righteous, and his ears are open to their cry" (34:15; cf. vv. 15–22). It does not take much inspection to become aware that the prayers and collections of prayers tend to come earlier in the Psalter, and the hymns of praise tend to come later. In this respect the Psalter as a whole reflects the movement to be found in the lament or prayer for help as a genre. That is, as the cry for help in each prayer moves from its complaint and lament features, including petition, often fairly extended (e.g., 3:1–4; 4:1–2; 6:1–7; 12:1–4; *22:1–21a*; etc.) to its expressions of confidence or assurance of a hearing and vows of thanksgiving (e.g., 3:4–6, 8; 4:7–8; 6:8–10; 10:14–18; *22:21b–31*; etc.), so also the Psalter makes a similar move on the macrocosmic level. Like the prayer for help itself, the Psalter as a whole gradually moves from the cry or prayer of the distressed and oppressed onward to the songs of praise and thanksgiving for God's steadfast love and acts of deliverance.

The Conclusion to the Psalter

While the sounds of crying do not disappear toward the end of the Psalter, it most clearly ends in extravagant praise, suggestive of the way of the righteous before God. That strong conclusion in praise and thanksgiving is evident in several ways that ring the changes on how the journey of faith is to come out. One of these is the character of Psalm 145 as both the conclusion to Book V of the Psalter (Pss. 107–145) and the beginning of the conclusion to the Psalter as a whole (Pss. 145–150). Many features of the psalm make this clear and tell the reader how things are to end, on heaven and on earth. Let me identify a few of them:

• The superscription of Psalm 145 is *tĕhillâ lĕdāwid*, "a hymn, of David." This is the last Davidic superscription and the only place in the Psalter where a psalm is called a "hymn." David's voice as both representative king and representative human creature—and he is both in the Psalter—has moved from prayer to praise. This heading serves both to provide a title for the Psalter as *tĕhillîm*, "hymns of praise," and to anticipate all that follows after this to the end of the Psalter: nothing but praise.

• If the Psalter can be construed as a declaration of the rule of the Lord over God's people, the nations, and the whole creation—a claim that starts at the beginning of the Psalter with Psalm 2 and provides its climax in Book IV in the Enthronement Psalms—that claim is now reaffirmed in Psalm 145 in the most concentrated language to be found in the Psalter, culminating with the declaration: "Your kingdom is an everlasting kingdom, and your dominion endures throughout all generations" (v.13; cf. vv. 1, 11–12). There is no doubt whose kingdom this is or that it has no end.

• Psalm 145 is framed by the declaration of its subject's intent to praise and bless (i.e., thank) God's name "forever and ever" (vv. 1–2 and 21). The goal of the psalmist, of human life, and of the Psalter is such never-ending praise and thanksgiving. It happens in this psalm, in the psalms preceding it, and in the psalms that follow. At the beginning and at the end of the psalm, the praise is "forever and ever" (3x), an echo of the previous doxologies (Pss. 41:13; 72:18–19; 89:52; 106:48) that end each of the first four books of the Psalter, but one that carries the doxology further. It is no longer "forever" or "from everlasting to everlasting" but "forever and ever" (v. 1), . . . "forever and ever" (v. 2), . . . "forever and ever" (v. 21). It does not take much to hear Handel's "Hallelujah Chorus" as one reads this psalm and the ones that follow. The church's frequent appropriation of that chorus to end its services, especially at occasions such as Christmas or Easter, is an ongoing expression of what happens at the end of the Psalter.

• Psalm 145 carries its concluding, emphatic, and totalizing move to the utter praise of God in another evident way: its repeated use of the adjective "all." In the second half of the psalm, verses 9–21, "all" or "every" appears sixteen times. All and everything everywhere shall know the Lord's steadfast love and render praise to the Lord. Nothing is outside of this.

• The final verse of Psalm 145 opens up the coda of praise that is found in the last five psalms and frames it in such a way that it moves from the praise by the individual psalmist's "I" (vv. 1 and 21a) to the praise by "all flesh" (v. 21b). That movement describes what happens in the final group of psalms, which begins with the praise by the individual "I" in Psalm 146:

> Praise the LORD, O my soul!
> I will praise the LORD as long as I live. (vv. 1b–2a)

And by the end, all flesh and all creation have been called to give praise to the Lord. The declaration at the end of Psalm 145 that "all flesh will bless his holy name forever and ever" (v. 21b) is picked up in the final verse of the Psalter—the last word, the bottom line: "Let everything that breathes praise the LORD!" (150:6).

The movement so described is central to the movement of prayer and faith as that is encountered in the Psalms. The experience of God's response and help evokes jubilant thanksgiving, at the center of which is the psalmist's testimony about what God has done for the supplicant. The personal experience and celebration of an individual can evoke, and is meant to evoke, the praise of the whole. The one who praises and gives thanks calls for all to praise and give thanks because of what God has done to help. It is the Psalter's form of what we call *testimony*. As the Psalter comes to its end, the testimony of all the Psalms calls forth the praise of everyone and everything—the individual (Ps. 146), Jerusalem-Zion (Ps. 147), creation (Ps. 148), God's people Israel (Ps. 149), and finally every musical instrument and every breathing creature (Ps. 150). This means that the many laments sounded throughout the Psalter are not the last word. The sound one hears at the end is not the lonely tears of the suffering human being but the music of praise reverberating throughout a world ruled by the Lord, who is gracious and merciful and whose ears are tuned to hear the cries of the hurt and the poor. The final outcome is God's saving help in all circumstances, and the Psalter is full of testimonies to that effect. The title of the book is *těhillîm*, "Hymns of praise" not *těpillôt*, "prayers for help." The concluding notes are entirely *těhillâ*, and they say now not only that lament is not the last word, but also that all the prayers have now become a form of praise. This book is a book of good news of great joy, and the community of God-fearers does not read or sing these psalms finally as complaint but as praise.

To Glorify and Enjoy God Forever

So it is that the Psalter ends up where the Catechism begins, with an unending chorus of praise to the Lord. The voices are everywhere: in nature, in Jerusalem, throughout Israel's story. "Let everything that breathes praise the LORD" is the final word of the Psalter. As Psalm 150 emphasizes, with its beginning and ending word occurring thirteen times in the psalm, our reason for being can be summed up in a single word: "*Hallelujah*." "*Praise the LORD*." That ascription of glory, that glorifying, is also an unending moment of joy. It is like a universe full of cheers reverberating in every corner and through all of time: *Hallelujah, hallelujah, hallelujah*. If the first psalm says the Psalter is there to teach us the way of the righteous, how we are to be and do, the final Psalm shows us how that way ends. The contribution of Psalm 2 to the whole is to let us know why it is that God is to be glorified: because the Lord reigns over all. If you want to know the character of that reign and why it merits praise and glory, then keep reading in the Psalter, such psalms as 82 and 86 and 103, indeed all of them.

Let us then pursue the matter one step further by asking: In the light of all this, where is the *joy* to be found? Where do we encounter or experience the enjoyment of God that is our chief end, our purpose and outcome as human beings? The Psalms suggest several answers to that question:

1. One answer the Psalms give repeatedly is *in the sanctuary*. This is evident in the frequent experience of yearning to be there, to spend time in the sanctuary, in the presence of the Lord. Thus in Psalm 27 we read:

> One thing I asked of the LORD,
>   that will I seek after:
> to live in the house of the LORD
>   all the days of my life,
> to behold the beauty of the LORD,
>   and to inquire in his temple. (v. 4)

As the verses that follow indicate, such a life in the temple is for divine protection:

> For he will hide me in his shelter
>   in the day of trouble;
> he will conceal me under the cover of his tent. (v. 5)

But the experience of seeking God's face, God's beauty, is in order to live a life of joy:

> Now my head is lifted up
>   above my enemies all around me,
> and I will offer in his tent
>   sacrifices with shouts of joy;
> I will sing and make melody to the LORD. (v. 6)

Similar words are sounded elsewhere and frequently in the Psalter:

> So I have looked upon you in the sanctuary,
>   beholding your power and glory. (63:2)

> Ascribe to the LORD glory and strength.
> Ascribe to the LORD the glory due his name. (96:7–8//29:1–2)

> And in the temple all say, "Glory!" (Ps. 29:9)

Or as Psalm 16 puts it, "In your presence there is fullness of joy" (v. 11). Similarly in Psalm 43:4:

> Then I will go to the altar of God,
>   to God my exceeding joy;
> and I will praise you with the harp,
>   O God, my God.

While such Psalm texts could be heaped up further, their force seems to be clear. They are the voices of those who find in their being in the sanctuary, in their coming to church, an encounter with the Lord that is the source of joy and delight. The psalmists implicitly raise before us the matter of whether that is where we find our highest joy and ask whether the experience of worship becomes for us an experience of God's beauty and presence, where doxology is truly the sound of joy and delight.

2. Ultimately I think that is the case and thus why, when we ask where human enjoyment of God may be found, the most obvious and unambiguous place is in *our music*. As the Psalter comes to an end in its call to the praise of the Lord, every breathing creature and every instrument breaks forth into nothing but praise:

Praise [the LORD] with trumpet sound;
  praise him with lute and harp!
Praise him with tambourine and dance;
  praise him with strings and pipe!
Praise him with clanging cymbals;
  praise him with loud clashing cymbals! (150:3–5)

The sound of praise is the sound of music, and the sound of music is the sound of joy. Once as a young boy I had some kind of angry encounter with one of my sisters, the details of which I cannot remember at all, only my fierce anger. Shortly after this encounter, while I was still stewing, I was told by my mother to practice the piano in preparation for the piano lesson coming up shortly. I can still remember trying desperately to hold on to my anger as I practiced and my genuine frustration as the anger slowly passed away. I wanted to keep it, but the music would not let the anger stay in my heart.

Nothing takes us closer to heaven, and nothing creates the experience of transcendence more than music. Fred Pratt Green says it well in his great hymn: "When in our music God is glorified, . . . it is as though the whole creation cried, 'Alleluia!'" Such joy can only be shared by God. I think that is something of what is meant by encountering the beauty of God in the sanctuary.

In the play *Amadeus*, Peter Shaffer dares to hear the music of glory and joy from the mind of God as Mozart says at one point:

"I tell you I want to write a finale lasting half an hour! A quartet becoming a quintet becoming a sextet. On and on, wider and wider— all sounds multiplying and rising together—and then together making a sound entirely new! . . . I bet that's how God hears the world. Millions of sounds ascending at once and rising in His ear to become an unending music, unimaginable to us!"[2]

3. If we ask where the joy in the Lord is to be found, we cannot forget what Calvin often noted: that *God's creation* is a *theater of glory* and the source of joy for all of us who are a part of it. Creation can be dangerous and messy, as we all know, but it never ceases to be a theater of glory. As Calvin put it, "Let us not be ashamed to take pious delight in the works of God open and manifest in this most beautiful theater."[3] I will mention only two psalms. Psalm 65 speaks for itself:

By your strength you established the mountains;
    you are girded with might.
You silence the roaring of the seas,
    the roaring of their waves,
    the tumult of the peoples.
Those who live at earth's farthest bounds are awed by your signs;
you make the gateways of the morning and the evening shout for joy.
You visit the earth and water it,
    you greatly enrich it;
The river of God is full of water;
    you provide the people with grain,
    for so you have prepared it.
You water its furrows abundantly,
    settling its ridges,
softening it with showers,
    and blessing its growth.
You crown the year with your bounty;
    your wagon tracks overflow with richness.
The pastures of the wilderness overflow,
    the hills gird themselves with joy,
the meadows clothe themselves with flocks,
    the valleys deck themselves with grain,
    they shout and sing together for joy. (vv. 6–13)

In the great poem of creation that is Psalm 104, the beauty and joy of creation is found in its order and the pleasure that it brings to the creatures, human and otherwise, who inhabit God's world. God made the waters to nourish the trees so that birds could inhabit them so that we can hear their songs. The word *śāmaḥ*, meaning "enjoy," "celebrate," "take pleasure in," is one of the words occurring most often in Psalm 104, clueing us in to joy and pleasure in creation as part of our being here. As the psalm comes to a conclusion, the shared joy of creature and Creator becomes explicit:

May the glory of the Lord endure forever;
    may the Lord rejoice [take pleasure] in his works. (v. 31)

And then the psalmist makes his own exclamation of joy: "for I rejoice [take pleasure] in the Lord" (v. 34b). In a very modern vein, the physicist-theologian John Polkinghorne echoes the psalmist when he writes: "Just as the rational transparency and wonderful order of the physical world become intelligible if they are seen as reflecting the Mind of the world's Creator, so human experiences of beauty can be understood as a sharing in the joy that God takes in creation."[4]

Finally, we cannot finish/complete our answer to the question Where do human beings find their enjoyment of God? without attending to the strong signals we are given in the introduction to the Psalter, Psalm 1, and the torah Psalms 19 and 119.[5] We have already noticed this dimension of the law as we find it in the Psalms, so we need only bring it to bear as part of the answer to our question: Where is the enjoyment of God to be found? Over and over these psalms tell us that our joy and delight are to be found *in the law*, in God's instruction. "The precepts of the LORD are right, rejoicing the heart," says Psalm 19:8. And in Psalm 119, this joy in the law/torah never ends: "I delight in the way of your decrees" (v. 14). "Your decrees are my delight" (v. 24). "Lead me in the path of your commandments, for I delight in it" (v. 35). "Your statutes have been my songs wherever I make my home" (v. 54). "Your decrees are . . . the joy of my heart" (v. 111). And so it goes, on and on.

In the holy place, in our music, in the theater of God's glory, and especially in God's instructing word—we are led to praise and to find the deepest enjoyment of the Lord who made us and meets us, who hears us and calls us. That is our chief end. And I take it that such a claim is not only about why we are here but also about where we are going. Certainly the theology of the Psalter propels us toward the end, right from the beginning. The image of the way has no meaning if it is not a path that leads somewhere. When Psalm 1 announces that the wicked shall not stand in the judgment, it is possible to read that completely within the judicial procedures of ancient Israel. But it is hard not to hear a word at the beginning about the way things will end. So the literary end of the Psalter seems to carry us to the end of our existence, engulfed forever in the glory and joy of the Lord.

Notes

Abbreviations

JSOTSup   Journal for the Study of the Old Testament: Supplement Series
LHB/OTS   Library of Hebrew Bible / Old Testament Studies

Introduction

1. In this regard, see two essays by Patrick D. Miller, "What Is a Human Being? The Anthropology of the Psalter 1," in *The Way of the Lord: Essays in Biblical Theology*, Forschungen zum Alten Testament 39 (Tübingen: Mohr Siebeck: 2004; repr., Wm. B. Eerdmans Publishing Co., 2007), 226–36; and "The Sinful and Trusting Creature: The Anthropology of the Psalter II," in ibid., 237–49.

Chapter 1: The Reality of God

1. *Time*, April 8, 1966.
2. Rolf A. Jacobson, *"Many Are Saying": The Function of Direct Discourse in the Hebrew Psalter*, JSOTSup 397 (London: T&T Clark International, 2004), 55.

Chapter 2: God among the Gods

1. See Patrick D. Miller, *Interpreting the Psalms* (Philadelphia: Fortress, 1986), 120–24.
2. John Dominic Crossan, *The Birth of Christianity: Discovering What Happened in the Years Immediately after the Execution of Jesus* (San Francisco; HarperSanFrancisco, 1998), 575; cf. J. Clinton McCann Jr., "The Single Most Important Text in the Entire Bible: Toward a Theology of the Psalms," in *Soundings in the Theology of Psalms: Perspectives and Methods in Contemporary Scholarship*, ed. Rolf Jacobson (Minneapolis: Fortress, 2011), 63–75.
3. James Luther Adams, "The Love of God," in *On Being Human Religiously: Selected Essays in Religion and Society*, ed. Max Stackhouse (Boston: Beacon Press, 1976), 96.
4. H. L. Ginsberg, *Kitvê Ûgārît* [Hebrew] (Jerusalem: The Bialik Foundation, 1936), 129ff.; cf. Frank M. Cross Jr. "Notes on a Canaanite Psalm in the Old Testament," *Bulletin of the American Schools of Oriental Research* 117 (1950): 19–21.

5. Cf. Aloysius Fitzgerald, "Note on Psalm 29," *Bulletin of the American Schools of Oriental Research* 215 (1974): 61–63.
6. Or "wise, understanding, and experienced," but the root of the last adjective (yd^c) is the same as in Ps. 82's "knowledge."
7. James Luther Mays, "The Center of the Psalms: 'The LORD Reigns' as Root Metaphor," in *The Lord Reigns: A Theological Handbook to the Psalms* (Louisville, KY: Westminster John Knox Press, 1994), 12–22; cf. Gerald Henry Wilson, *The Editing of the Hebrew Psalter*, Society of Biblical Literature Dissertation Series 76 (Chico, CA: Scholars Press, 1985).

Chapter 3: The Body of God

1. For recent discussion of divine embodiment, see Benjamin D. Sommer, *The Bodies of God and the World of Ancient Israel* (Cambridge: Cambridge University Press, 2009); and S. Tamar Kamionkowski and Wonil Kim, eds., *Bodies, Embodiment, and Theology of the Hebrew Bible*, LHB/OTS [formerly JSOTSup] 465 (New York: T&T Clark, 2010).
2. Choon-Leong Seow, "Face *pānîm*," *Dictionary of Deities and Demons in the Bible*, ed. K. van der Toorn, B. Becking, and P. W. van der Horst, 2nd ed. (Grand Rapids: Wm. B. Eerdmans Publishing Co., 1999), 323.
3. Ibid.
4. Ibid.
5. Note the parallelism of God's spirit and God's face.
6. Dennis Overbye, reporting for *The New York Times* on May 17, 2010, http://www.nytimes.com/2010/05/18/science/space/18cosmos.html?_r=0.
7. I have discussed these images in other contexts, such as "The Sovereignty of God," in *The Hermeneutical Quest: Essays in Honor of James Luther Mays on His Sixty-fifth Birthday*, ed. Donald G. Miller (Pittsburgh: Pickwick Press, 1986), 129–44; repr. in Patrick D. Miller, *Israelite Religion and Biblical Theology*, JSOTSup 267 (Sheffield: Sheffield Academic Press, 2000), 406–21; idem, "God the Warrior: A Problem in Biblical Interpretation and Apologetics," *Interpretation* 19 (1965): 39–46; repr. in idem, *Israelite Religion and Biblical Theology*, 356–64; idem, *The Religion of Ancient Israel*, Library of Ancient Israel (Louisville, KY: Westminster John Knox Press, 2000), 6–12.
8. I assume that is what was involved when my father once reduced his counsel to me about how to act as a young man to the words "Remember who you are."
9. Karl Barth, *Church Dogmatics*, II/1 (Edinburgh: T&T Clark, 1957), 480.
10. On the heavens and the earth, see Michael Welker, *Creation and Reality* (Minneapolis: Fortress Press, 1999), 33–44.

Chapter 4: Maker of Heaven and Earth

1. For further discussion of this rubric and its connection to the theme of creation in the Psalms, see James Luther Mays, "'Maker of Heaven and Earth': Creation in the Psalms," in *God Who Creates: Essays in Honor of W. Sibley Towner*, ed. William P. Brown and S. Dean McBride Jr. (Grand Rapids: Wm. B. Eerdmans Publishing Co., 2000), 75–86; repr. in idem, *Preaching and Teaching the Psalms*, edited by Patrick D. Miller and Gene M. Tucker (Louisville, KY: Westminster John Knox Press, 2006), 41–50.
2. William Brown, *Seeing the Psalms: A Theology of Metaphor* (Louisville, KY: Westminster John Knox Press, 2002), 156.

3. Patrick D. Miller, "What Is a Human Being? The Anthropology of Scripture," in *What About the Soul? Neuroscience and Christian Anthropology*, ed. Joel B. Green (Nashville: Abingdon, 2004) 68; repr. in idem, *The Way of the Lord*, 231.

4. For a discussion of connections in another dimension, that is, between creation and covenant, see Patrick D. Miller, "Creation and Covenant," in *Biblical Theology: Problems and Perspectives: In Honor of J. Christiaan Beker*, ed. Steven J. Kraftchick, Charles D. Myers Jr., and Ben C. Ollenburger (Nashville: Abingdon Press, 1995), 155–68; repr. in idem, *Israelite Religion and Biblical Theology*, 470–91.

5. Verses 23–24 of Ps. 102 are a brief return to the lament of the psalm's earlier part.

6. Cf. Patrick D. Miller, "The Psalter as a Book of Theology," in *Biblical Texts in Community: The Psalms in Jewish and Christian Traditions*, ed. Harold W. Attridge and Margot E. Fassler (Leiden: Brill; Atlanta: Society of Biblical Literature, 2003), 87–89; repr. in idem, *The Way of the Lord*, 214–25; and see idem, "Rethinking the First Article of the Creed," in *Theology Today* 61 (2005): 499–508; repr. in idem, *Theology Today: Reflections on the Bible and Contemporary Life* (Louisville, KY: Westminster John Knox Press, 2006), 124–31.

Chapter 5: "To Glorify Your Name"

1. This lecture, delivered in Heidelberg, Germany, was originally published as "'Deinem Namen die Ehre': Die Psalmen und die Theologie des Alten Testaments," in *Evangelische Theologie* 67 (2007): 32–42; used by permission; cf. Gerhard von Rad, *Old Testament Theology*, trans. D. M. G. Stalker, 2 vols. (New York: Harper, 1962–65).

2. See chapter 7.

3. One encounters a similar perspective in the dialogues of the book of Job, yet in the context of the whole of the book, the initiative is clearly from the divine world. That is also the case in various ways with the psalms and other prayers as they react to what they have experienced of divine judgment or abandonment.

4. See, e.g., Bernd Janowski, *Konfliktgespräche mit Gott: Eine Anthropologie der Psalmen* (Neukirchen: Neukirchener Verlag, 2003; 2nd ed., 2006; 3rd ed., 2010; 4th ed., 2013); trans. Armin Siedlecki as *Arguing with God: A Theological Anthropology of the Psalms* (Louisville, KY: Westminster John Knox, 2013); and three essays by Patrick D. Miller: "What Is a Human Being? The Anthropology of the Psalter I," in *The Way of the Lord*, 226–36; "The Sinful and Trusting Creature: The Anthropology of the Psalter II," in *The Way of the Lord*, 237–49; and "Heaven's Prisoners: The Lament as Christian Prayer," in *Lament: Reclaiming Practices in Pulpit, Pew, and Public Square*, ed. Sally A. Brown and Patrick D. Miller (Louisville, KY: Westminster John Knox, 2005), 15–26.

5. On the image of YHWH as refuge in the redaction of the Psalter, see Jerome Creach, *Yahweh as Refuge and the Editing of the Hebrew Psalter*, JSOTSup 217 (Sheffield: Sheffield Academic Press, 1996).

6. There is much we do not know about the cultic activity in which the prayers are set and whether different elements of the prayers might represent different stages or moments in the total experience. Hugh G. M. Williamson has suggested, e.g., that the lament or prayer for help as a whole may have been articulated only after the experience of deliverance had taken place; see his essay "Reading the Lament Psalms Backwards," in *A God So Near: Essays on Old Testament Theology in Honor of Patrick D. Miller*, ed. Brent A. Strawn and Nancy R. Bowen (Winona Lake, IN: Eisenbrauns, 2003), 3–15.

7. Walter Brueggemann, *Theology of the Old Testament: Testimony, Dispute, Advocacy* (Minneapolis: Fortress, 1997); cf. idem, *Old Testament Theology: Essays on Structure, Theme, and Text*, ed. Patrick D. Miller (Minneapolis: Fortress Press, 1992), 1–44.

8. Hermann Spieckermann, "God's Steadfast Love: Towards a New Conception of Old Testament Theology," *Biblica* 81 (2000): 305–27; trans. as "Die Liebeserklärung Gottes: Entworf einer Theologie des Alten Testaments," in Spieckermann, *Gottes Liebe zu Israel*, Forschungen zum Alten Testament 33 (Tübingen: Mohr Siebeck, 2001), 197–223; cf. in the same volume his earlier essay "'Barmherzig und gnädig ist der Herr . . . ,'" 3–19. For a more extended treatment of *ḥesed* in the Old Testament, see Katharine Doob Sakenfeld, *The Meaning of* Hesed *in the Hebrew Bible: A New Inquiry*, Harvard Semitic Monographs 17 (Missoula, MT: Scholars Press, 1978).

9. Spieckermann, "God's Steadfast Love," 315.

10. Over half of all occurrences of *ḥesed* and over half of all its occurrences with reference to God are in the Psalter.

11. Spieckermann, "God's Steadfast Love," 311.

12. The dimension of promise is large in the Psalter. Many commentators have suggested eschatological dimensions to the Psalms, and David Mitchell has proposed an eschatological program underlying the whole Psalter (*The Message of the Psalter: An Eschatological Programme in the Book of Psalms*, JSOTSup 252 [Sheffield: Sheffield Academic Press, 1997]). Clearly many psalms anticipate the future reign of God. One of the psalms that reflects the emphasis that Spieckermann has provided would be the shortest one of all, Ps. 117. There the principal message is about how the *ḥesed* of the Lord has overwhelmed and conquered Israel so thoroughly and how the *ʾĕmet* of the Lord can be counted on to continue into the future. The *ḥesed* and *ʾĕmet* of God have dominated the past and will continue to dominate the future. It is particularly astounding, but fits with other notes one hears, that the *ḥesed* of God is something that may legitimately be put forth as evoking the praise and exaltation of all the nations as well. See, e.g., the testimony of the nations in Ps. 126:2.

13. For specific dismissive comments on Ps. 86 from such scholars as Luis Alonso-Schökel, Bernhard Duhm, and Hermann Gunkel, see Frank-Lothar Hossfeld and Erich Zenger, *Psalms 2*, Hermeneia (Minneapolis: Fortress, 2005), 369 n.1.

14. "The creativity of the author of Psalm 86 is shown in the fact that, on the one hand, he has combined conventionalized Psalms language in such a way that Psalm 86 appears as a summary of 'Davidic' psalms, especially the partial compositions Psalms 40–41 and 69–71, 72, which conclude the two 'Davidic Psalters,' Psalms 3–41 and 51–71, 72, and that on the other hand, by adopting the Sinai theology of Exodus 33–34, he gives the psalm an overall horizon that then acquires further dimensions of meaning in the context of the Psalter" (ibid., 369); cf. Jürgen Vorndran, "*Alle Völker werden kommen*": *Studien zu Psalm 86*, Bonner biblische Beiträge 133 (Münster: Univ. Diss., 2000–2001; Berlin: Philo, 2002), cited by Hossfeld and Zenger but unavailable to me at the time of writing.

15. See the comment of James Luther Mays: "It has been written so that whoever uses the psalm prays with *a sustained concentration on the character of God and the identity of the one who prays*" (*Psalms*, Interpretation [Louisville, KY: John Knox Press, 1994], 278; emphasis mine).

16. The only other Deuteronomic references to crying out to the Lord are in Deut. 15:9 and 24:15. In both cases, they are examples of the appeal that the poor and needy can

make to God when they have been oppressed. See Norbert Lohfink, "Poverty in the Laws of the Ancient Near East and of the Bible," *Theological Studies* 52 (1991): 46.

17. For discussion of this formula, see Patrick D. Miller, *They Cried to the Lord: The Form and Theology of Biblical Prayer* (Minneapolis: Fortress Press, 1994), 193–94.

18. Hossfeld and Zenger, *Psalms 2*, 373.

19. Wilson, *The Editing of the Hebrew Psalter*; James L. Mays, "The Center of the Psalms: 'The Lord Reigns' as Root Metaphor," in *Language, Theology, and the Bible: Essays in Honour of James Barr*, ed. Samuel E. Balentine and John Barton (Oxford: Clarendon Press, 1994), 231–46; repr. in idem, *The Lord Reigns*, 12–22.

20. Erich Zenger, "Der Psalter als Buch: Beobachtungen zu seiner Entstehung, Komposition und Funktion," in *Der Psalter in Judentum und Christentum*, ed. Erich Zenger, Herders biblische Studien 18 (Freiburg im Breisgau: Herder, 1998), 47, AT.

21. Richard Kratz, "Die Tora Davids: Psalm 1 und die doxologische Funfteilung des Psalter," *Zeitschrift für Theologie und Kirche* 93 (1996): 11.

22. Among other studies, see Kratz, "Die Tora Davids"; the essay by Bernd Janowski, "Freude an der Tora: Psalm 1 als Tor zum Psalter," *Evangelische Theologie* 67 (2007): 18–31; and Patrick D. Miller, "The Beginning of the Psalter," in *The Shape and Shaping of the Psalter*, ed. J. C. McCann, JSOTSup 159 (Sheffield: JSOT Press, 1993), 83–92; repr. in idem, *Israelite Religion and Biblical Theology*, 269–78.

23. See Patrick D. Miller, "Deuteronomy and Psalms: Evoking a Biblical Conversation," *Journal of Biblical Literature* 118 (1999): 3–18; repr. in Miller, *Israelite Religion and Biblical Theology*, 318–36.

24. In this regard, see Kratz, "Die Tora Davids," 1–2; and Bernd Janowski, "Die 'Kleine Biblia': Zur Bedeutung der Psalmen für eine Theologie des Alten Testaments," in Zenger, *Der Psalter in Judentum und Christentum*, 381–83.

Chapter 6: Tender Mercies

1. Brian Brock, *Singing the Ethos of God: On the Place of Christian Ethics in Scripture* (Grand Rapids: Wm. B. Eerdmans Publishing Co., 2007), 74.

2. The answer to question 4, "What is God?" in the Westminster Shorter Catechism.

3. For extended discussion of this point with regard to the Old Testament generally, see J. Gerald Janzen, *At the Scent of Water: The Ground of Hope in the Book of Job* (Grand Rapids: Wm. B. Eerdmans Publishing Co., 2009), chap. 2. My discussion of this matter is heavily indebted to Janzen's work.

4. Ibid., 36.

5. Walter Brueggemann, "Bounded by Obedience and Praise: The Psalms as Canon," in idem, *The Psalms and the Life of Faith*, ed. Patrick D. Miller (Minneapolis: Fortress Press, 1995), 189–213.

Chapter 7: The First Catechism Question and Psalter Theology

1. In this regard, see esp. Wilson, *The Editing of the Hebrew Psalter*.

2. Peter Shaffer, *The Collected Plays of Peter Shaffer* (New York: Harmony Books, 1982), 527.

3. John Calvin, *Institutes of the Christian Religion* 1.14.20 (ed. John T. McNeill, trans. Ford Lewis Battles, Library of Christian Classics 20 [Philadelphia: Westminster Press, 1960], 1:179).

4. John Polkinghorne, *Theology in the Context of Science* (New Haven: Yale University Press, 2009), 95.

5. In this regard, see Beverly Roberts Gaventa, "To Glorify God and Enjoy God Forever: A Place for Joy in Reformed Readings of Scripture," in *Reformed Theology: Identity and Ecumenicity II; Biblical Interpretation in the Reformed Tradition*, ed. Wallace M. Alston Jr. and Michael Welker (Grand Rapids: Wm. B. Eerdmans Publishing Co., 2007), 107–15.

Scripture Index

Psalms (*continued*)
139:7	31
139:7–10	35
139:17–18	13
139:23–24	13
140:12	89
143:7	33
145	91–93
145:13	45
145:21b	93
146–50	89, 92–93
146:1b–2a	93
146:5–6	53, 55
146:5–10	56
146:6	47
146:7–10	26
146:8–9	89
147	56–58
148	49, 53, 55
148:5	50, 57
148:8	57
150	94
150:3–5	96
150:6	53, 93

Proverbs
| | 2 |

Ecclesiastes
| | 2 |

Isaiah–Malachi
| | 64 |

Isaiah
6:8	21
11:4	12
11:9	12
40:6–8	78
41:21–29	21
54:7–8	76
57:16	76

Jeremiah
3:12	76
5:1	9–10
22:15–17	11
30:22	66
33:11	84

Lamentations
| 3:55–57 | 40 |
| 5:16 | 80 |

Hosea
4:1b	11
4:6	10–11
6:6	11
11:3–4	38
11:9	37

NEW TESTAMENT

Matthew
| 1:21–23 | 46 |
| 27:41–43 | 7 |

Mark
| 2:1–12 | 80 |

John
1	58
1:3–5	33–34
1:9	33–34
1:14	46
8:12	34

Acts
| 9:3–5 | 34 |

Romans
| 8:39 | 78 |

2 Corinthians
| 4:6 | 34 |

Ephesians
| 1:12 | 50 |
| 1:14 | 50 |

Philippians
| 2:6–11 | 45–46 |
| 2:7 | 7 |

Hebrews
| 10:31 | 23 |

1 John
| 1:5 | 33 |

Subject Index

fool on absence or noninvolvement of
God, 2–9
knowledge of God, 10–16
question on death of God (1960s
movement), 1, 22
righteous
on existence of God, 5–10
God's love of, 56
God's tests of, 14–15
hope of, 88
justice for, 25–27
and law of God, 89–90, 98
prayer of, 34, 91
support for poor and weak by, 89
ways of, 91, 94
wicked versus, 8, 88–90
righteousness of God, 10–12, 26–27,
55–56, 74, 77–78, 88
rock imagery, 6, 8, 37, 63
Romans, Letter to, 78
royal psalms, 86–87. *See also* kingship/
rulership
rulership. *See* kingship/rulership

šāmah (enjoy), 97
sanctuary, 94–96
šāpāt (to judge), 24
Sarah, 3
Satan, 10
Saul. *See* Paul
Seow, Leong, 32
Shaffer, Peter, 96
Shema, 68
Sheol, 67
shepherd image, 36
sickness, 79–83
sins, 75, 77–82, 88. *See also* forgiveness of
God; wicked/enemy
sleep and awakening, 22–23
Solomon, 43
space in relation to God, 42–44. *See also*
dwelling place of God
speech of God, 39–41
Spieckermann, Hermann, 64, 102n12
ṣrp (test), 14–15
storm god, 20

suffering
of humans, 79–81, 83
of Jesus, 7, 40
See also poor and oppressed

tabernacle, 42
těhillâ (hymn of praise), 92, 93
temple, 42–44, 87, 94–95
temporality and God, 44–46
těmûnâ (form), 37, 38
Ten Commandments, 11, 38, 68
tender mercies. *See* mercy of God
Tender Mercies, 71–72
těpillâ (prayer), 91. *See also* prayer for help
testimony, 93
Tetragrammaton, 19–20, 39
thanksgiving psalms
aspects of God's being in, xii, 83–84
as conclusion of Psalter, 91–98
existence of God and, 8
on God as judge, 26
on goodness and love of God, 67
for love of God, 84
praise and, 73, 83, 92, 93
and prayers for help, 91
on speech of God, 41
on universal dimension of God's works,
67–68
theodicy. *See* reality of God
theological language, 30–31
Theology of the Old Testament
(Brueggemann), 63
Tillich, Paul, 30
time in relation to God, 44–46
Time magazine, 1
ṭôb (good), 67. *See also* goodness
Torah, 64, 68, 69, 89
transience. *See* mortality
tree imagery, 90
trust in God, xii, 63, 66, 82

voice of God, 37, 39–41
Von Rad, Gerhard, 61, 63

warrior image, 37
waters of the earth, 52, 54, 55, 57, 83, 97

CPSIA information can be obtained at www.ICGtesting.com
Printed in the USA
LVOW13s2347061113

360235LV00002B/5/P

9 780664 239275